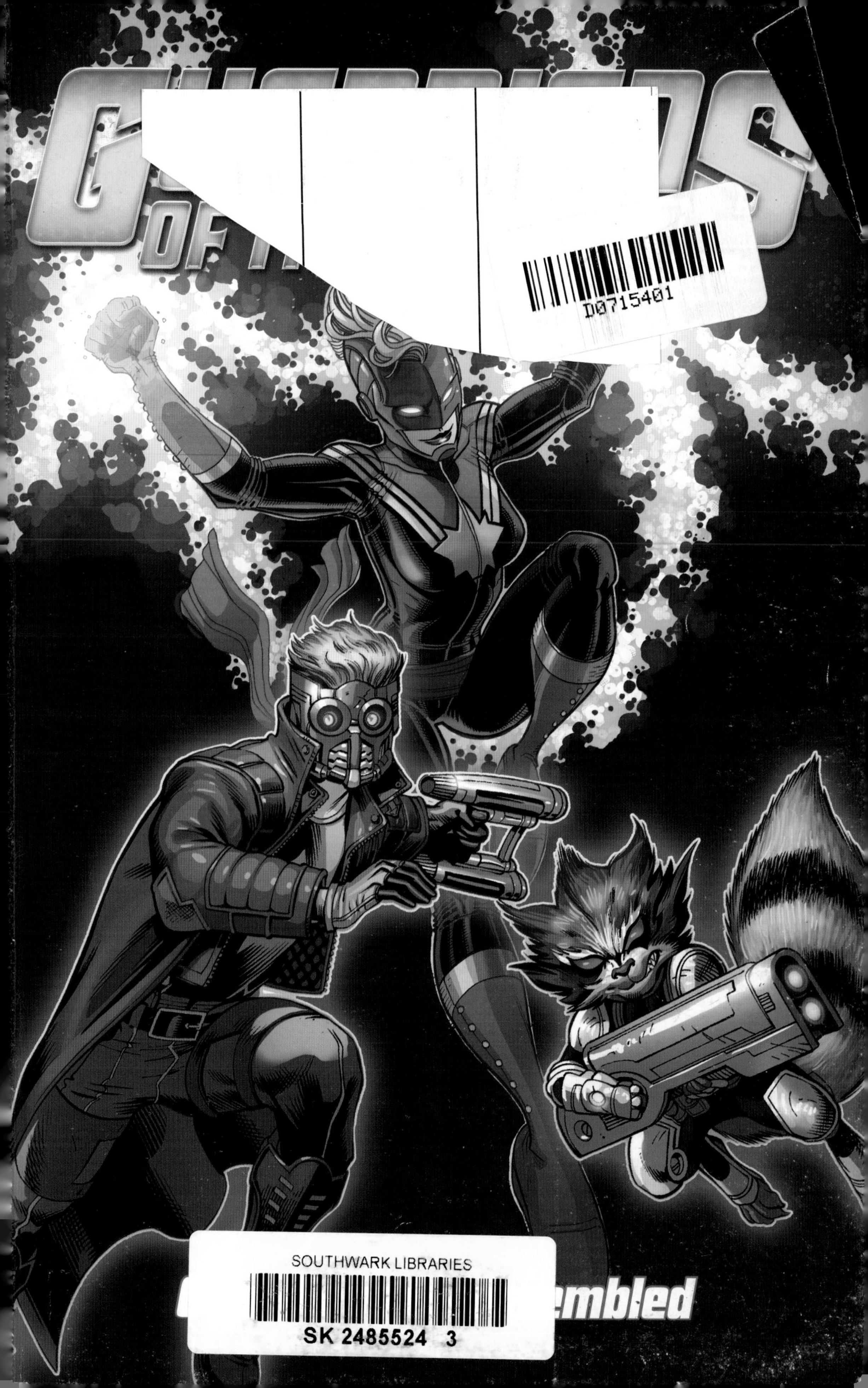

GUARDIANS OF THE GALAXY

GUARDIANS DISASSEMBLED

WRITER: BRIAN MICHAEL BENDIS

PENCILERS: NICK BRADSHAW WITH JASON MASTERS, TODD NAUK, CAMERON STEWART, DAVID MARQUEZ & MICHAEL OEMING

INKERS: NICK BRADSHAW WITH SCOTT HANA, CAMERON STEWART, WALDEN WONG, JASON MASTERS, DAVID MARQUEZ, MICHAEL OEMING & TODD NAUK

LETTERS: VIRTUAL CALLIGRAPHY'S CORY PETIT

COLOURS: JUSTIN PONSOR, MORRY HOLLOWELL, EDGAR DELGADO, JOSÉ VILLARRUBIA & JASON KEITH

ASSISTANT EDITOR: XANDER JAROWEY

EDITORS: MIKE MARTS WITH STEPHEN WACKER & ELLIE PYLE

EDITOR IN CHIEF: AXEL ALONSO

CHIEF CREATIVE OFFICER: JOE QUESADA

ANGELA COCREATED BY: TODD MCFARLANE & NEIL GAIMAN

COVERS #14, 15 AND 16: NICK BRADSHAW & JUSTIN PONSOR

COVER #17: ED MCGUINNESS, MARK FARMER & JUSTIN PONSOR

VENOM: REBIRTH

WRITER: DAN SLOTT
PENCILERS: PAULO SIQUEIRA & RONAN CLIQUET DE OLIVEIRA
INKERS: PAULO SIQUEIRA, ROLAND PARIS & GREG ADAMS
LETTERS: VIRTUAL CALLIGRAPHY'S JOE CARAMAGNA
COLOURS: FABIO D'AURIA
ASSISTANT EDITOR: ELLIE PYLE
EDITOR: STEPHEN WACKER

GROOT'S TALE

WRITER: ANDY LANNING
PENCILER: PHIL JIMENEZ
INKER: LIVESAY
LETTERS: VIRTUAL CALLIGRAPHY'S CORY PETIT
COLOURS: ANTONIO FABEL
CONSULTING EDITOR: ELLIE PYLE   EDITOR:
EXECUTIVE EDITOR: MIKE MA

CAPTAIN MARVEL

WRITER: KELLY SUE DECONNICK
ARTIST: DEXTER SOY
COVER ART: ED MCGUINNESS, DEXTER VINES & JAVIER RODRIGUEZ
LETTERS: VIRTUAL CALLIGRAPHY'S JOE CARAMAGNA
ASSISTANT EDITOR: ELLIE PYLE
EDITOR: STEPHEN WACKER
CAPTAIN MARVEL COSTUME DESIGNED BY: JAMIE MCKELVIE

FIGHT FOR THE FUTURE

WRITER: DAN ABNETT
ARTIST: GERARDO SANDOVAL
COLOURS: RACHELLE ROSENBERG
LETTERS: VIRTUAL CALLIGRAPHY'S JOE CARAMAGNA
ASSISTANT EDITOR: ELLIE PYLE
EDITOR: STEPHEN WACKER

Do you have any comments or queries about this grap[...] Panini/Marvel Graphic Novels.

MIX
Paper from responsible sources
FSC® C016466

PREVIOUSLY...

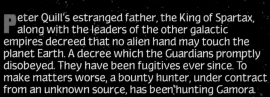

Peter Quill's estranged father, the King of Spartax, along with the leaders of the other galactic empires decreed that no alien hand may touch the planet Earth. A decree which the Guardians promptly disobeyed. They have been fugitives ever since. To make matters worse, a bounty hunter, under contract from an unknown source, has been hunting Gamora.

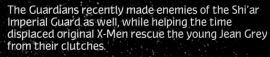

The Guardians recently made enemies of the Shi'ar Imperial Guard as well, while helping the time displaced original X-Men rescue the young Jean Grey from their clutches.

Meanwhile, the warrior Angela has found herself transplanted from her own universe through some error in the space-time continuum. Unidentifiable as any known species, she must now determine her place and purpose in the galaxy.

MARVEL GRAPHIC NOVEL

FREE COMIC BOOK DAY

(GUARDIANS OF THE GALAXY) #1

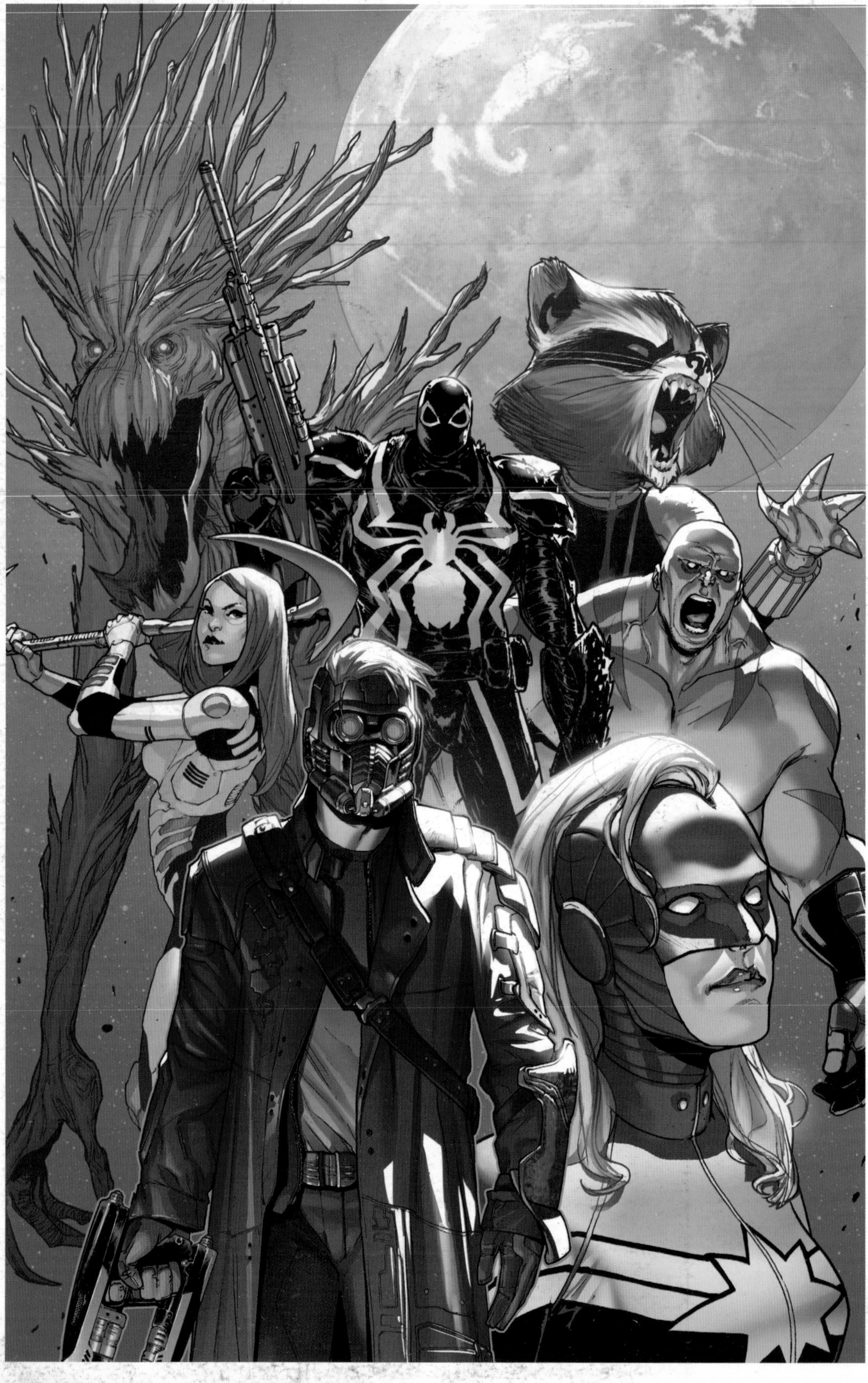

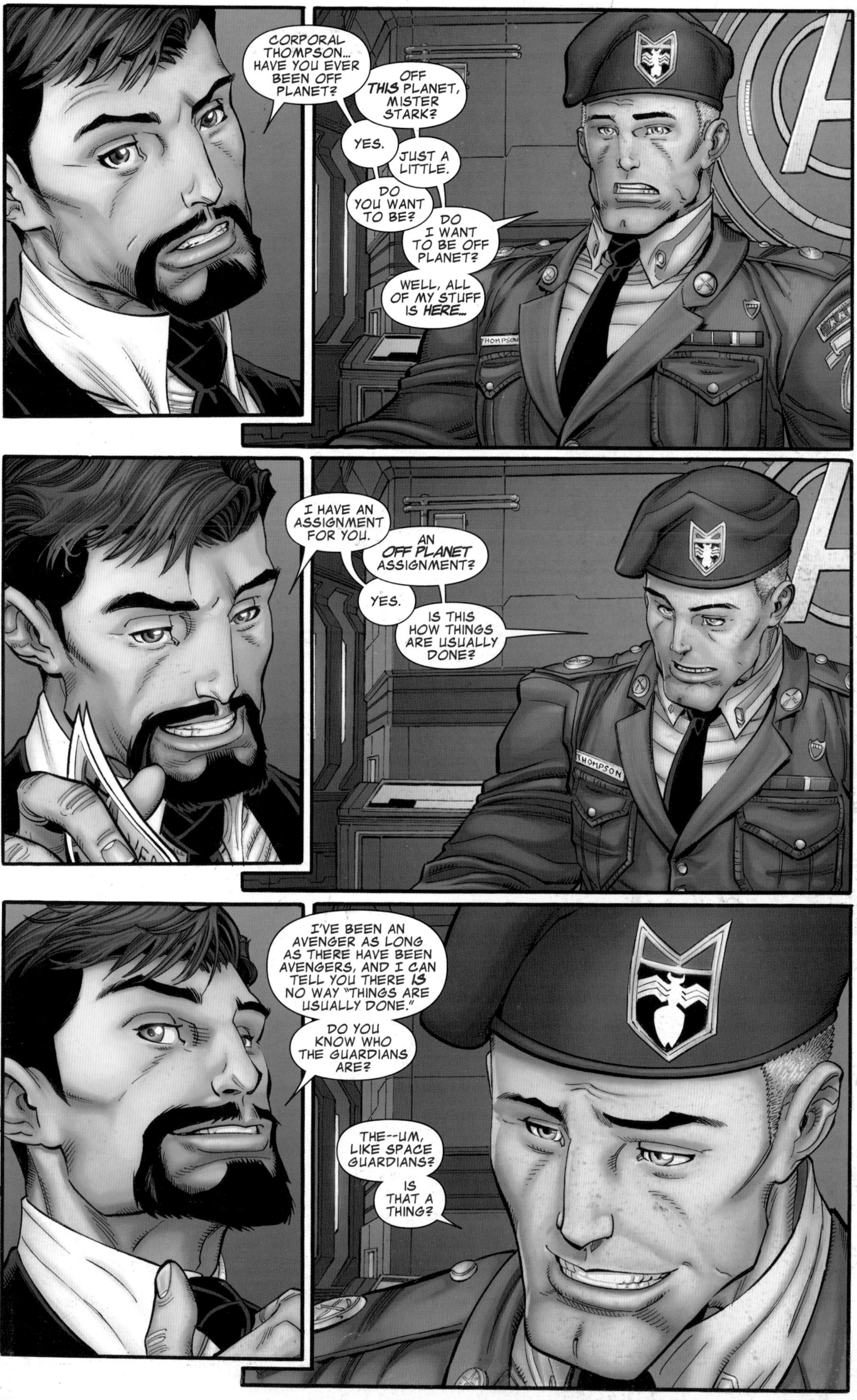
CORPORAL THOMPSON... HAVE YOU EVER BEEN OFF PLANET?
OFF THIS PLANET, MISTER STARK?
YES.
JUST A LITTLE.
DO YOU WANT TO BE?
DO I WANT TO BE OFF PLANET?
WELL, ALL OF MY STUFF IS HERE...
THOMPSON
I HAVE AN ASSIGNMENT FOR YOU.
AN OFF PLANET ASSIGNMENT?
YES.
IS THIS HOW THINGS ARE USUALLY DONE?
THOMPSON
I'VE BEEN AN AVENGER AS LONG AS THERE HAVE BEEN AVENGERS, AND I CAN TELL YOU THERE IS NO WAY "THINGS ARE USUALLY DONE."
DO YOU KNOW WHO THE GUARDIANS ARE?
THE--UM, LIKE SPACE GUARDIANS?
IS THAT A THING?

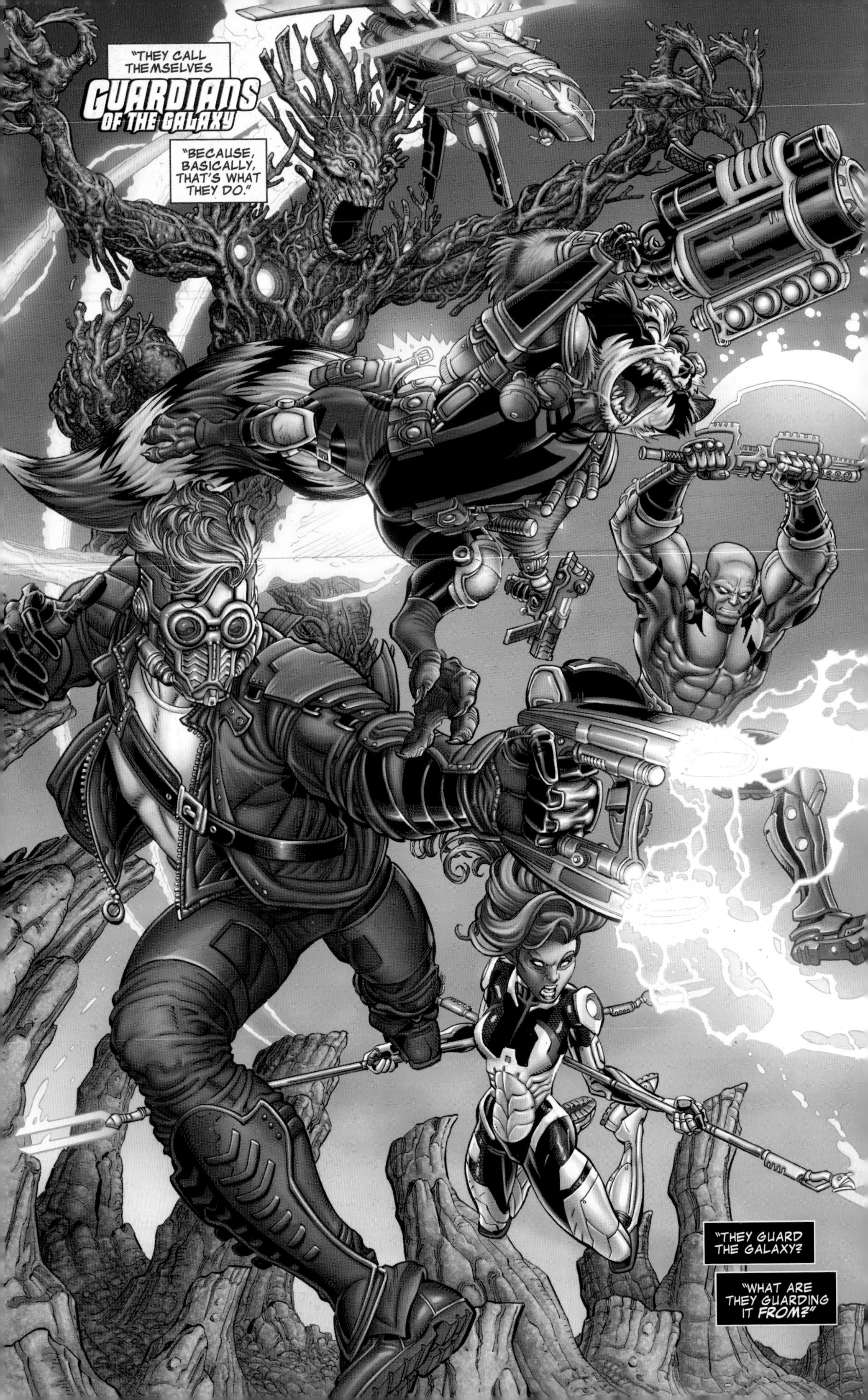
"THEY CALL THEMSELVES
GUARDIANS OF THE GALAXY
"BECAUSE, BASICALLY, THAT'S WHAT THEY DO."
"THEY GUARD THE GALAXY?
"WHAT ARE THEY GUARDING IT FROM?"

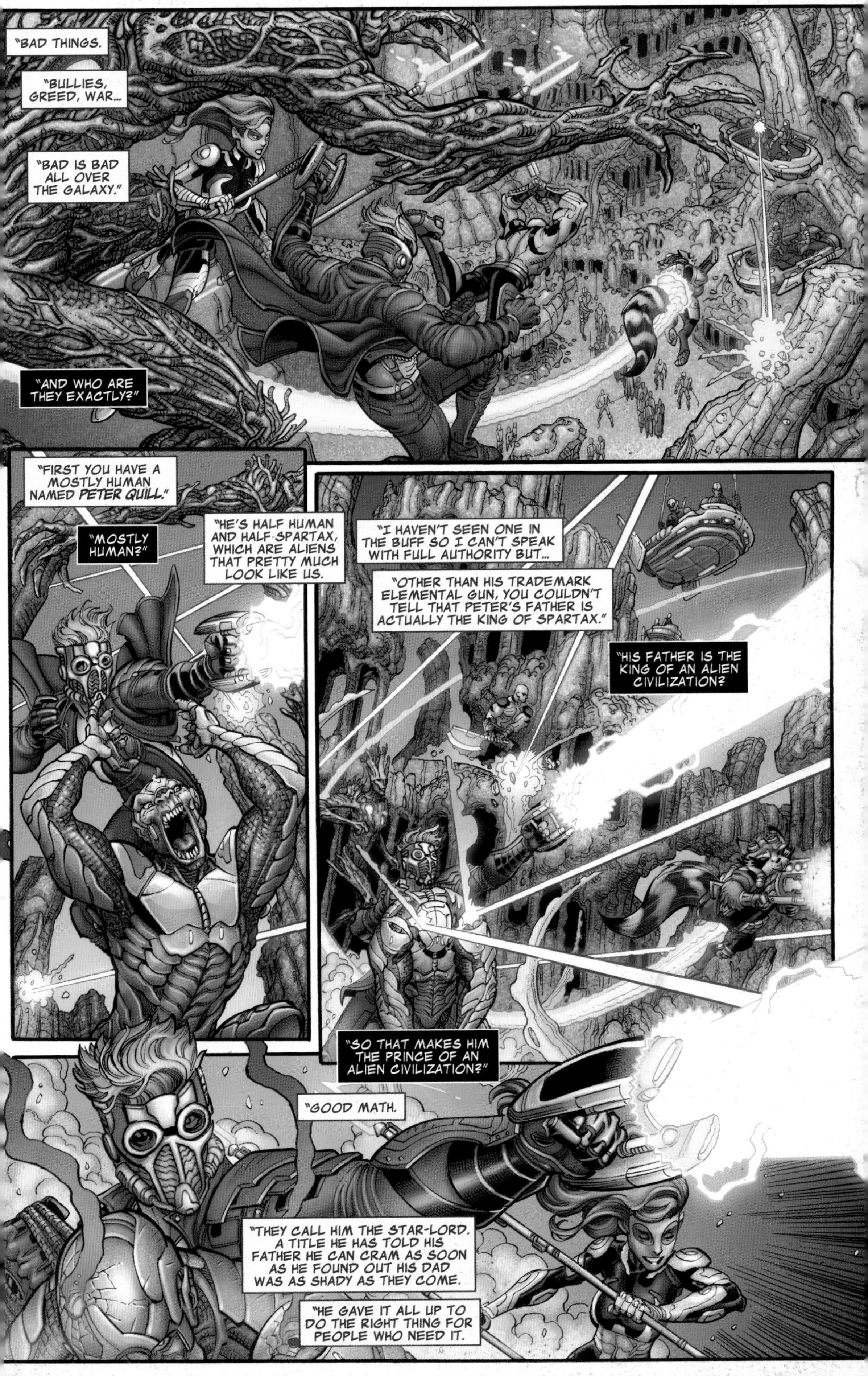
"BAD THINGS.
"BULLIES, GREED, WAR...
"BAD IS BAD ALL OVER THE GALAXY."
"AND WHO ARE THEY EXACTLY?"
"FIRST YOU HAVE A MOSTLY HUMAN NAMED PETER QUILL."
"MOSTLY HUMAN?"
"HE'S HALF HUMAN AND HALF SPARTAX, WHICH ARE ALIENS THAT PRETTY MUCH LOOK LIKE US.
"I HAVEN'T SEEN ONE IN THE BUFF SO I CAN'T SPEAK WITH FULL AUTHORITY BUT...
"OTHER THAN HIS TRADEMARK ELEMENTAL GUN, YOU COULDN'T TELL THAT PETER'S FATHER IS ACTUALLY THE KING OF SPARTAX."
"HIS FATHER IS THE KING OF AN ALIEN CIVILIZATION?
"SO THAT MAKES HIM THE PRINCE OF AN ALIEN CIVILIZATION?"
"GOOD MATH.
"THEY CALL HIM THE STAR-LORD. A TITLE HE HAS TOLD HIS FATHER HE CAN CRAM AS SOON AS HE FOUND OUT HIS DAD WAS AS SHADY AS THEY COME.
"HE GAVE IT ALL UP TO DO THE RIGHT THING FOR PEOPLE WHO NEED IT.

"AND THEN THERE IS ROCKET..."

"WHO LOOKS A LOT LIKE AN EARTH RACCOON."

"I'M SORRY?"

"BUT YOU ABSOLUTELY DO NOT CALL HIM A RACCOON!"

"IN FACT, YOU WOULD BE VERY WISE TO NOT EVEN USE THAT WORD IN FRONT OF HIM.

"HE TOLD ME THAT THE LAST GUY WHO CALLED HIM--"

"TOLD YOU? TOLD YOU, AS IN HE CAN SPEAK?"

"ALL HE DOES IS SPEAK.

"AND I HAVE TO SAY THIS TALKING, GENETICALLY ENGINEERED NOT-RACCOON IS JUST ABOUT THE MOST TECH SAVVY SON OF-A-GUN I'VE EVER BEEN AROUND, AND I'VE BEEN AROUND ALL OF THEM.

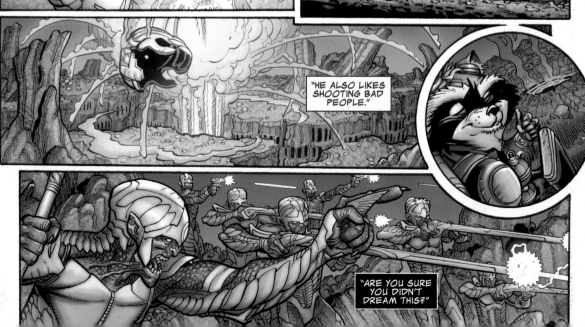

"HE ALSO LIKES SHOOTING BAD PEOPLE."

"ARE YOU SURE YOU DIDN'T DREAM THIS?"

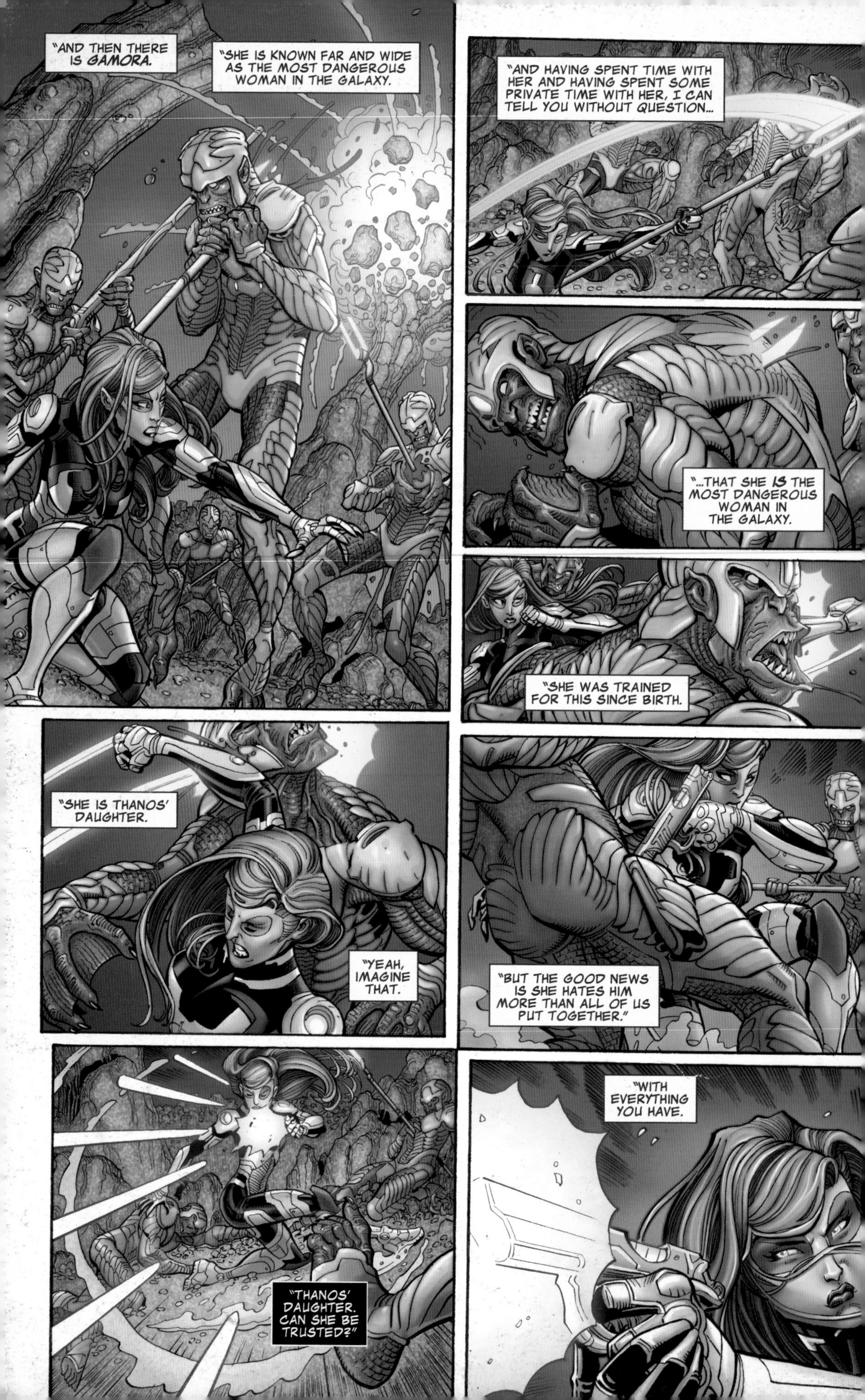
"AND THEN THERE IS GAMORA.
"SHE IS KNOWN FAR AND WIDE AS THE MOST DANGEROUS WOMAN IN THE GALAXY.
"AND HAVING SPENT TIME WITH HER AND HAVING SPENT SOME PRIVATE TIME WITH HER, I CAN TELL YOU WITHOUT QUESTION...
"...THAT SHE IS THE MOST DANGEROUS WOMAN IN THE GALAXY.
"SHE WAS TRAINED FOR THIS SINCE BIRTH.
"SHE IS THANOS' DAUGHTER.
"YEAH, IMAGINE THAT.
"BUT THE GOOD NEWS IS SHE HATES HIM MORE THAN ALL OF US PUT TOGETHER."
"THANOS' DAUGHTER. CAN SHE BE TRUSTED?"
"WITH EVERYTHING YOU HAVE.

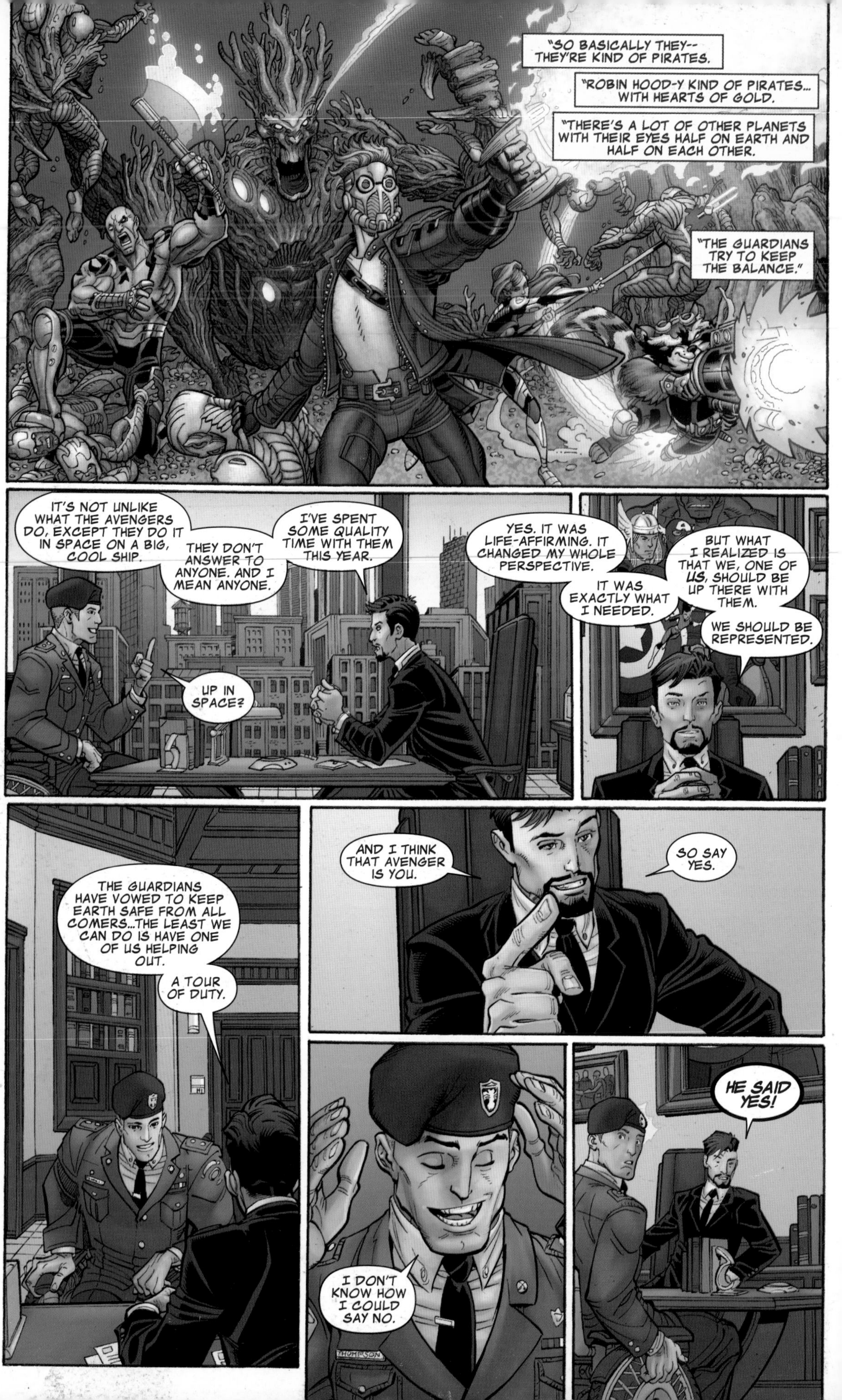
"SO BASICALLY THEY-- THEY'RE KIND OF PIRATES.
"ROBIN HOOD-Y KIND OF PIRATES... WITH HEARTS OF GOLD.
"THERE'S A LOT OF OTHER PLANETS WITH THEIR EYES HALF ON EARTH AND HALF ON EACH OTHER.
"THE GUARDIANS TRY TO KEEP THE BALANCE."
IT'S NOT UNLIKE WHAT THE AVENGERS DO, EXCEPT THEY DO IT IN SPACE ON A BIG, COOL SHIP.
THEY DON'T ANSWER TO ANYONE. AND I MEAN ANYONE.
I'VE SPENT SOME QUALITY TIME WITH THEM THIS YEAR.
UP IN SPACE?
YES. IT WAS LIFE-AFFIRMING. IT CHANGED MY WHOLE PERSPECTIVE.
IT WAS EXACTLY WHAT I NEEDED.
BUT WHAT I REALIZED IS THAT WE, ONE OF US, SHOULD BE UP THERE WITH THEM.
WE SHOULD BE REPRESENTED.
THE GUARDIANS HAVE VOWED TO KEEP EARTH SAFE FROM ALL COMERS...THE LEAST WE CAN DO IS HAVE ONE OF US HELPING OUT.
A TOUR OF DUTY.
AND I THINK THAT AVENGER IS YOU.
SO SAY YES.
I DON'T KNOW HOW I COULD SAY NO.
HE SAID YES!

I AM GROOT.

CHARMING WEAPONRY.

OKAY! NOW WE'RE TALKING.

I'VE SEEN YOUR KIND BEFORE. WHERE HAVE I SEEN YOUR KIND BEFORE?

WELL, THAT WENT WELL.

AND HERE'S A LITTLE SOMETHING FOR YOU, PETER...

JUST IN CASE.

A PRECAUTION.

I REALLY DON'T THINK YOU'LL NEED IT.

BUT...I AM MISTER JUST-IN-CASE.

JUST IN CASE YOU RUN INTO ANY UNFORESEEN SYMBIOTE TROUBLE.

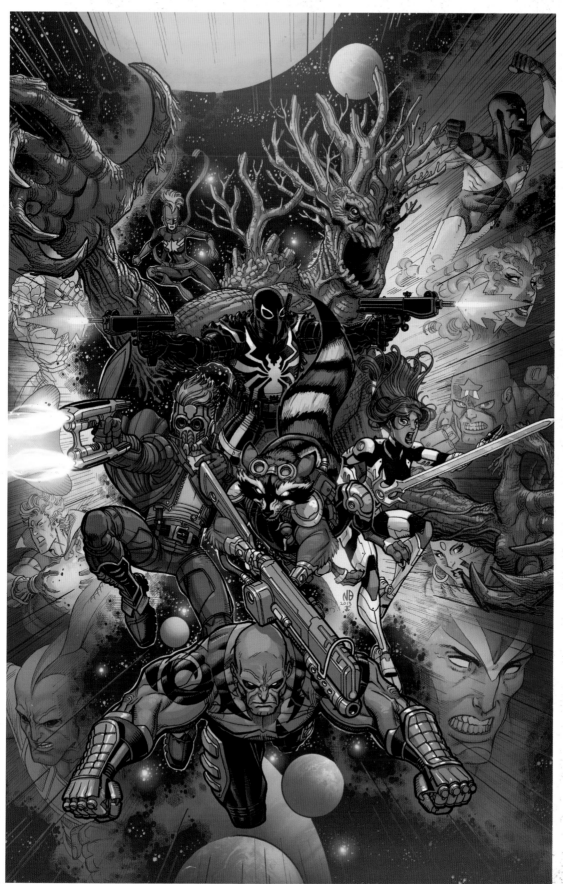

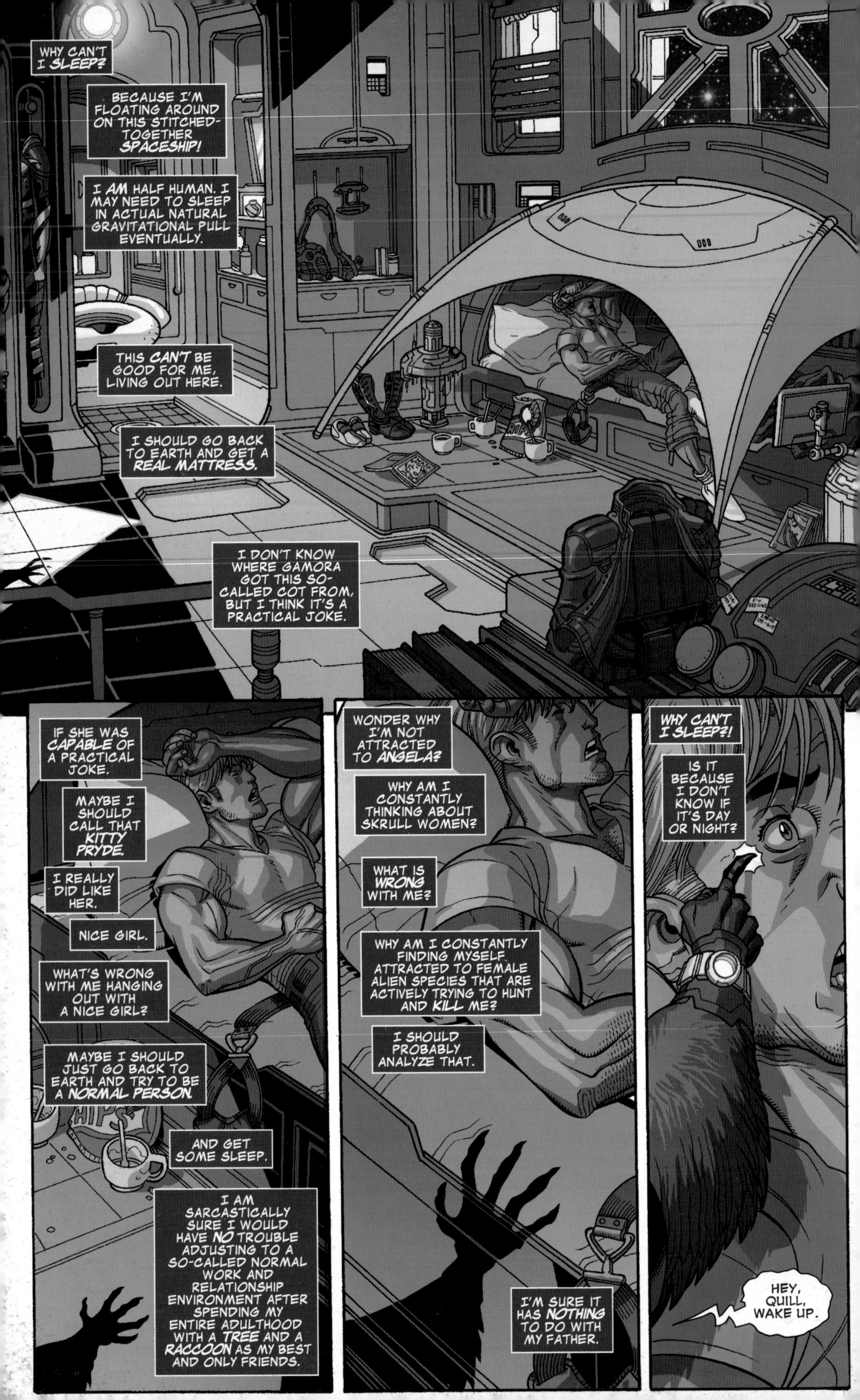
WHY CAN'T I SLEEP?
BECAUSE I'M FLOATING AROUND ON THIS STITCHED-TOGETHER SPACESHIP!
I AM HALF HUMAN. I MAY NEED TO SLEEP IN ACTUAL NATURAL GRAVITATIONAL PULL EVENTUALLY.
THIS CAN'T BE GOOD FOR ME, LIVING OUT HERE.
I SHOULD GO BACK TO EARTH AND GET A REAL MATTRESS.
I DON'T KNOW WHERE GAMORA GOT THIS SO-CALLED COT FROM, BUT I THINK IT'S A PRACTICAL JOKE.
IF SHE WAS CAPABLE OF A PRACTICAL JOKE.
MAYBE I SHOULD CALL THAT KITTY PRYDE.
I REALLY DID LIKE HER.
NICE GIRL.
WHAT'S WRONG WITH ME HANGING OUT WITH A NICE GIRL?
MAYBE I SHOULD JUST GO BACK TO EARTH AND TRY TO BE A NORMAL PERSON.
AND GET SOME SLEEP.
I AM SARCASTICALLY SURE I WOULD HAVE NO TROUBLE ADJUSTING TO A SO-CALLED NORMAL WORK AND RELATIONSHIP ENVIRONMENT AFTER SPENDING MY ENTIRE ADULTHOOD WITH A TREE AND A RACCOON AS MY BEST AND ONLY FRIENDS.
WONDER WHY I'M NOT ATTRACTED TO ANGELA?
WHY AM I CONSTANTLY THINKING ABOUT SKRULL WOMEN?
WHAT IS WRONG WITH ME?
WHY AM I CONSTANTLY FINDING MYSELF ATTRACTED TO FEMALE ALIEN SPECIES THAT ARE ACTIVELY TRYING TO HUNT AND KILL ME?
I SHOULD PROBABLY ANALYZE THAT.
I'M SURE IT HAS NOTHING TO DO WITH MY FATHER.
WHY CAN'T I SLEEP?!
IS IT BECAUSE I DON'T KNOW IF IT'S DAY OR NIGHT?
HEY, QUILL, WAKE UP.

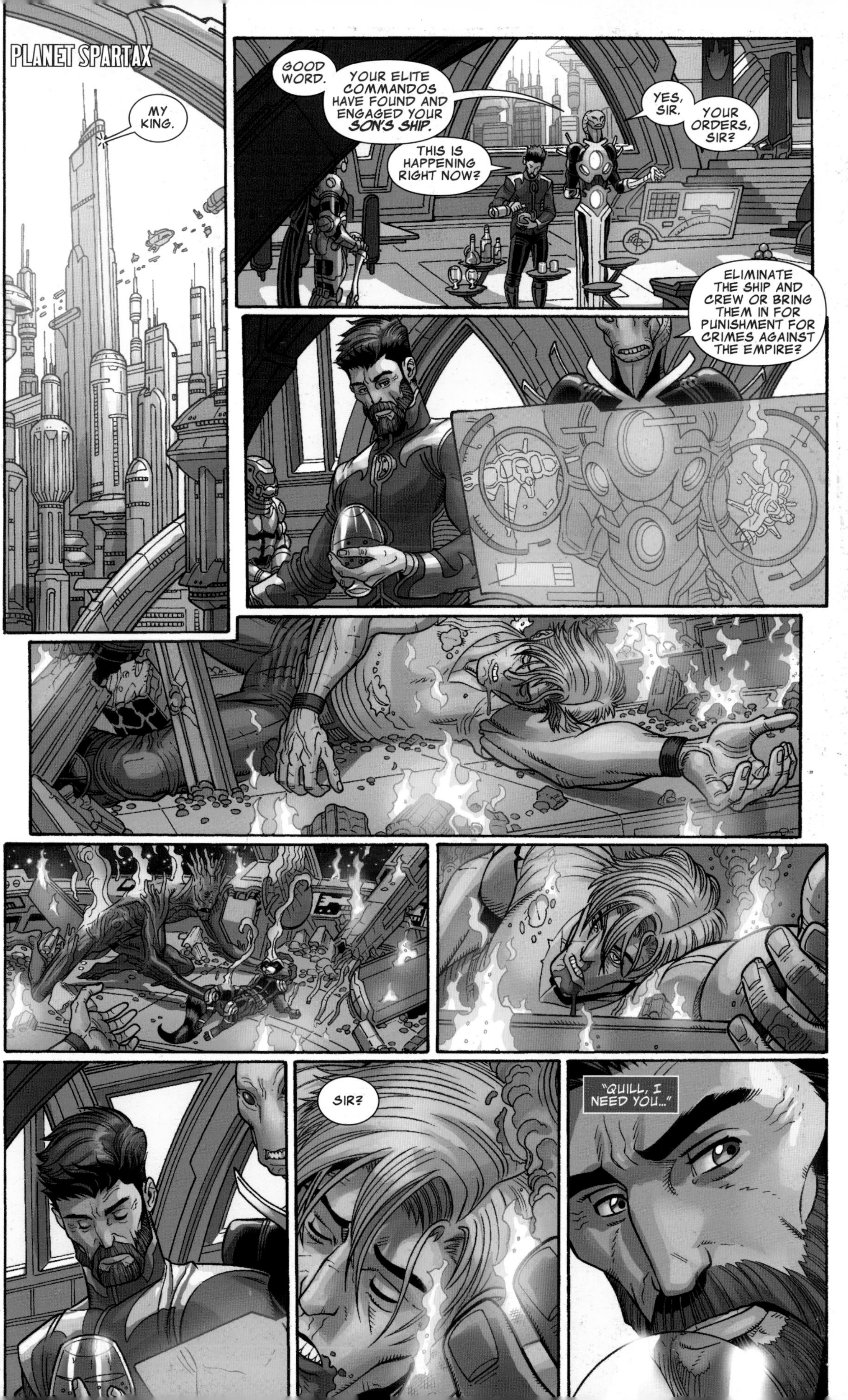
PLANET SPARTAX
MY KING.
GOOD WORD.
YOUR ELITE COMMANDOS HAVE FOUND AND ENGAGED YOUR SON'S SHIP.
THIS IS HAPPENING RIGHT NOW?
YES, SIR.
YOUR ORDERS, SIR?
ELIMINATE THE SHIP AND CREW OR BRING THEM IN FOR PUNISHMENT FOR CRIMES AGAINST THE EMPIRE?
SIR?
"QUILL, I NEED YOU..."

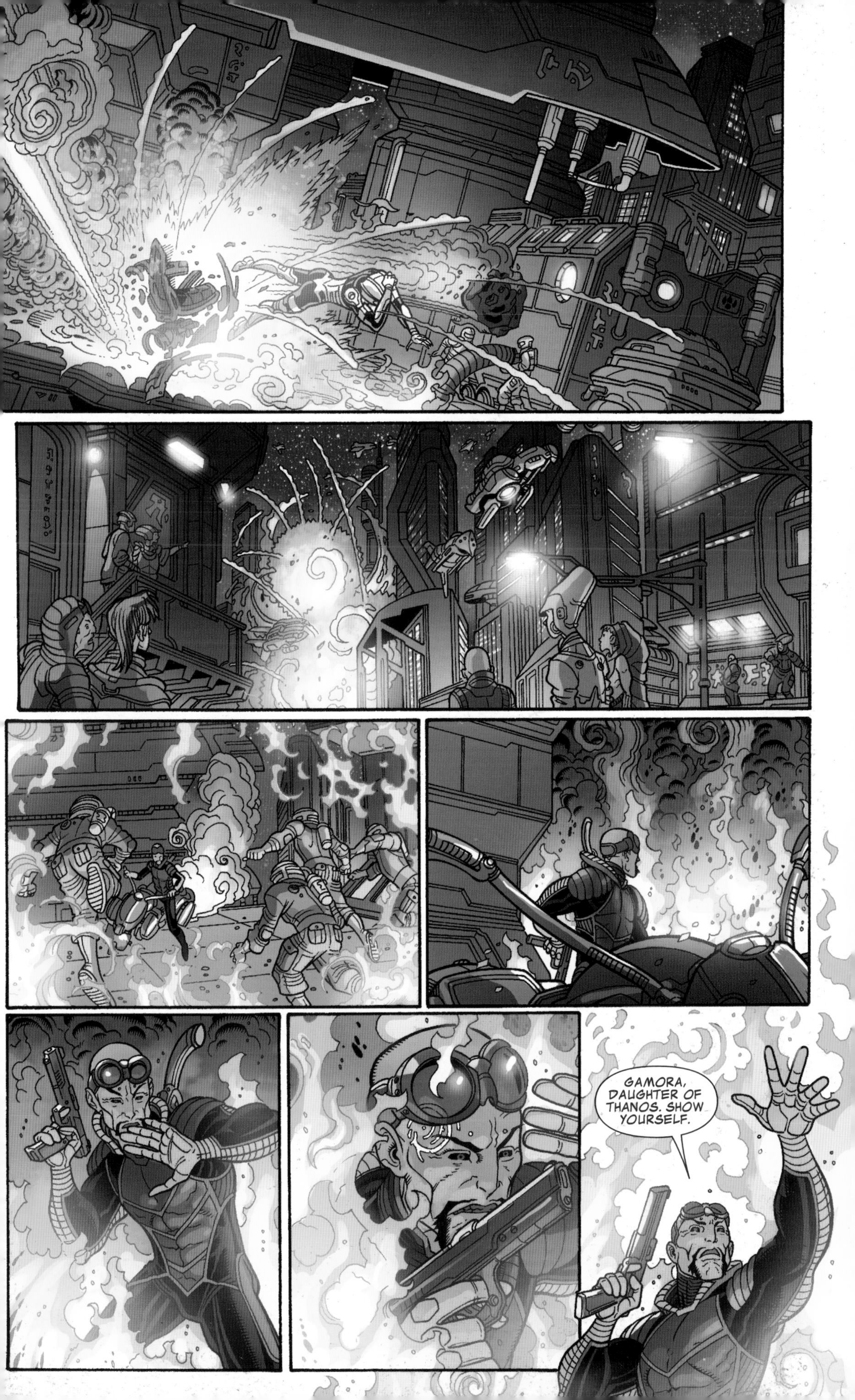
GAMORA, DAUGHTER OF THANOS. SHOW YOURSELF.

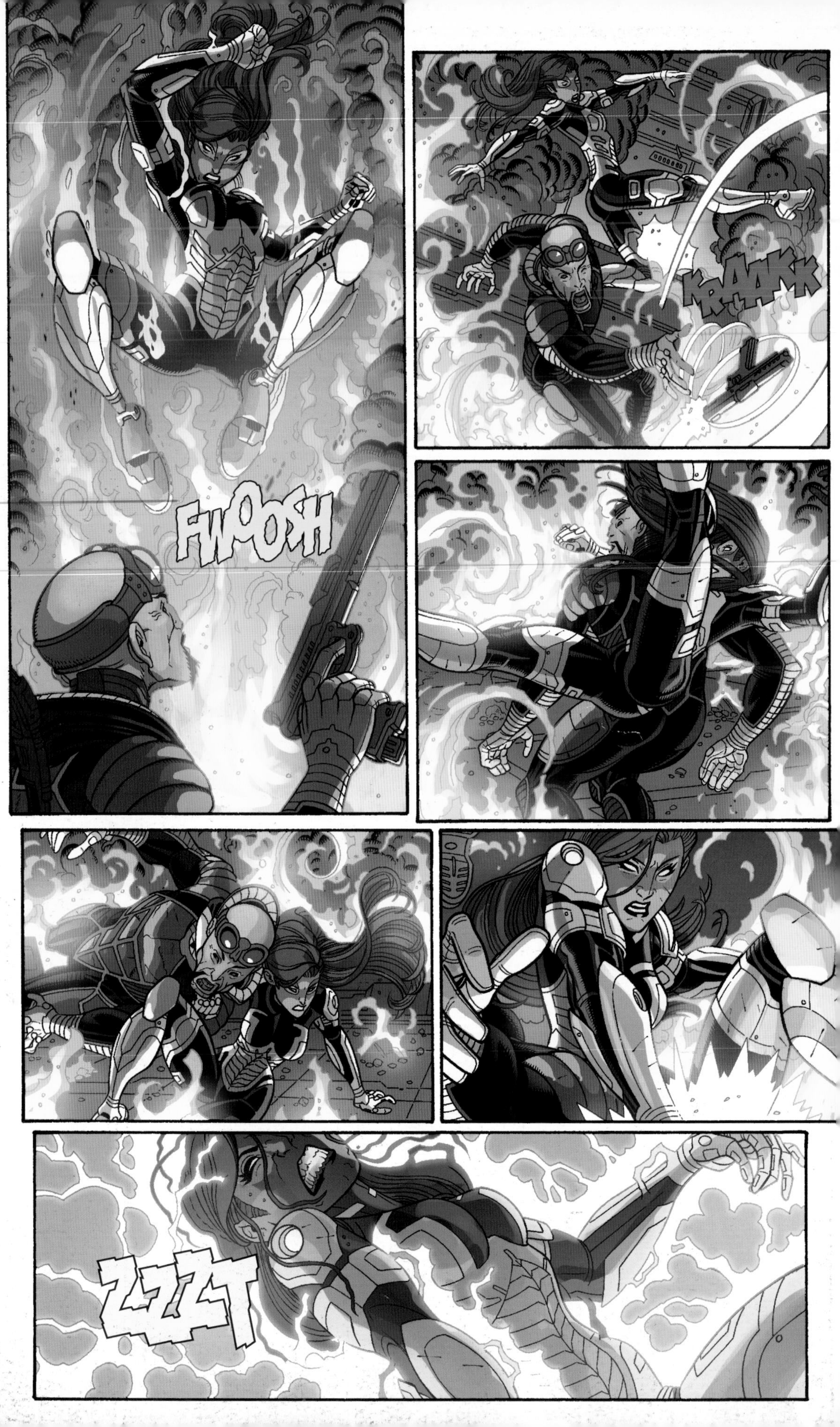
FWOOSH
KRAAKK
ZZZT

NOW I SEE WHY YOU KEEP HIM AROUND.

HE'S FUNNY.

LET'S SEE.

WE DON'T WANT TO GIVE HIM ANYTHING *TOO* DANGEROUS.

UM...

...THE SYMBIOTE PLANET?

WE *WANT* DANGEROUS.

RIGHT?

UM...

...YES?

OFF THIS PLANET.

I STILL CAN'T *BELIEVE* I'M NOT ON THE ONE I LIVE ON.

WHAT DID THAT, WHATEVER THAT WAS BACK THERE, MEAN ABOUT ME AND MY--?

HE IS A CRAKILI AND HE IS A FOOL.

I'M--HEY, I'M *ASKING* YOU.

DO YOU ALL KNOW SOMETHING ABOUT MY SYMBIOTE THAT I *DON'T KNOW*?

I'M ASKING, BECAUSE I LEFT EVERYTHING IN MY LIFE BEHIND ON EARTH TO COME OUT HERE AND HELP YOU BE GUARDIANS OF THE GALAXY.

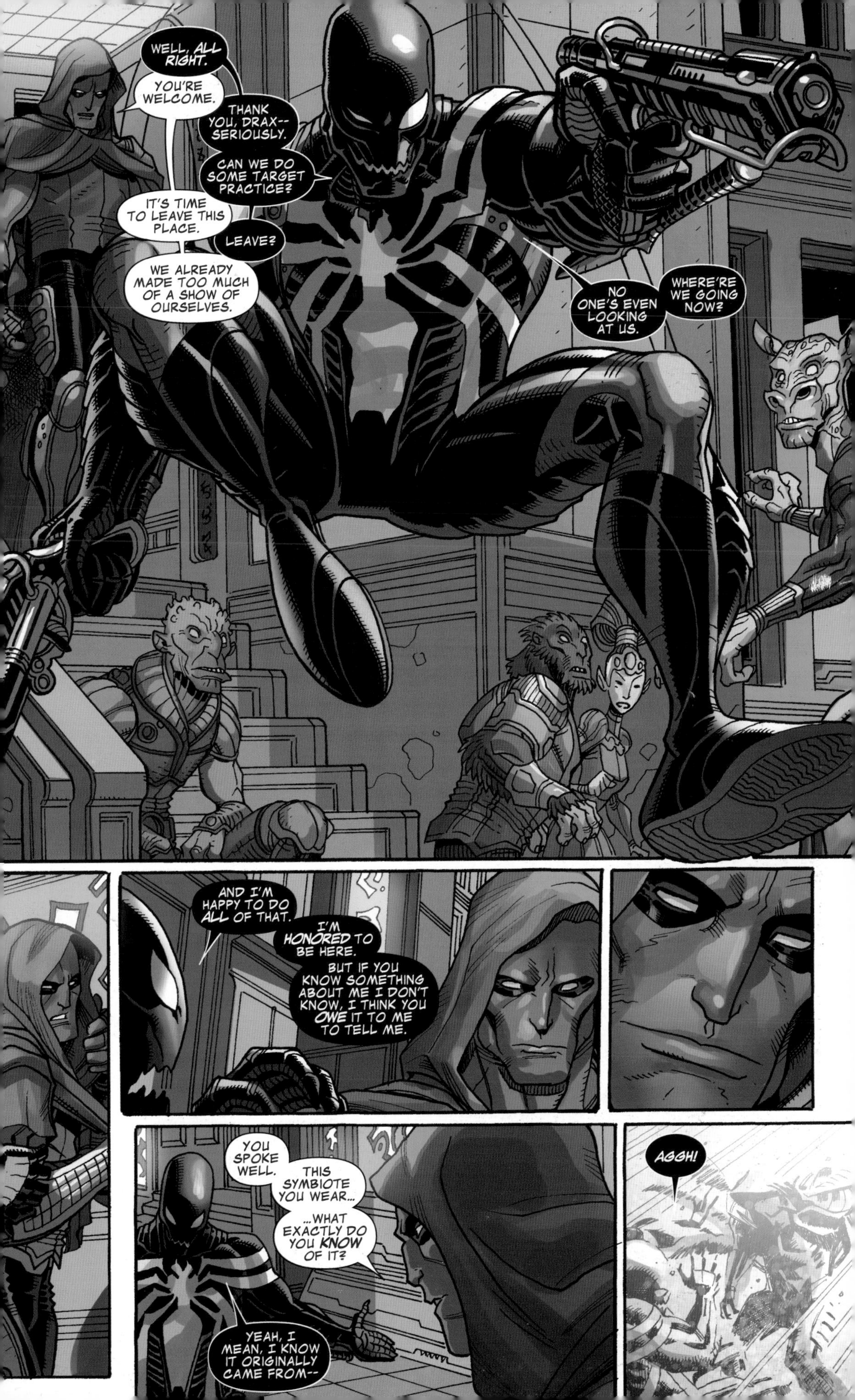
WELL, ALL RIGHT.
YOU'RE WELCOME.
THANK YOU, DRAX-- SERIOUSLY.
CAN WE DO SOME TARGET PRACTICE?
IT'S TIME TO LEAVE THIS PLACE.
LEAVE?
WE ALREADY MADE TOO MUCH OF A SHOW OF OURSELVES.
NO ONE'S EVEN LOOKING AT US.
WHERE'RE WE GOING NOW?
AND I'M HAPPY TO DO ALL OF THAT.
I'M HONORED TO BE HERE.
BUT IF YOU KNOW SOMETHING ABOUT ME I DON'T KNOW, I THINK YOU OWE IT TO ME TO TELL ME.
YOU SPOKE WELL.
THIS SYMBIOTE YOU WEAR...
...WHAT EXACTLY DO YOU KNOW OF IT?
YEAH, I MEAN, I KNOW IT ORIGINALLY CAME FROM--
AGGH!

UH, DRAX?

GYAAARRGGHH!

DROP HIM!

SNEEEEEEEEE

SNEEEEEEEE

KSHROOM

NNAAAGGHH!

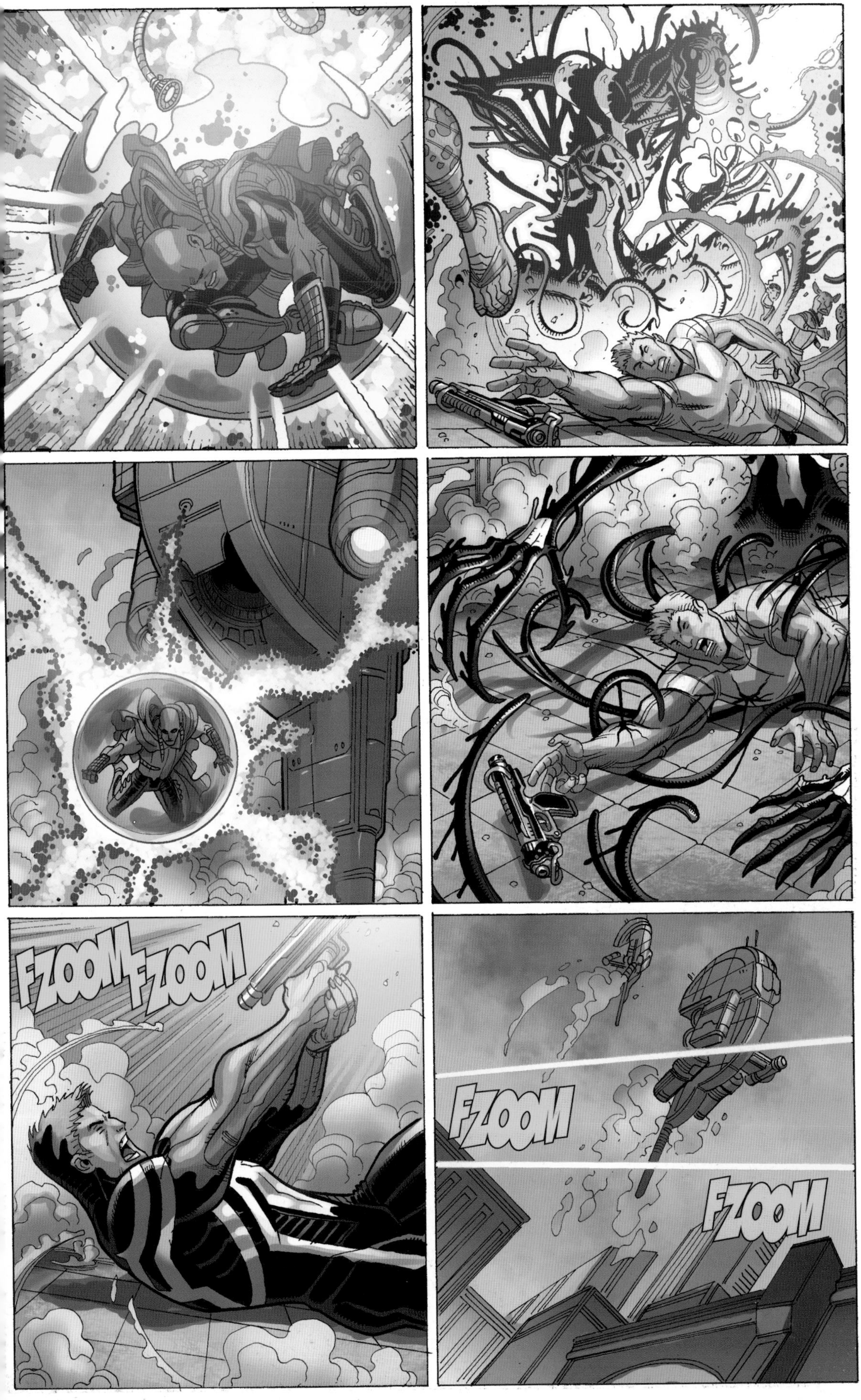
FZOOM FZOOM
FZOOM
FZOOM

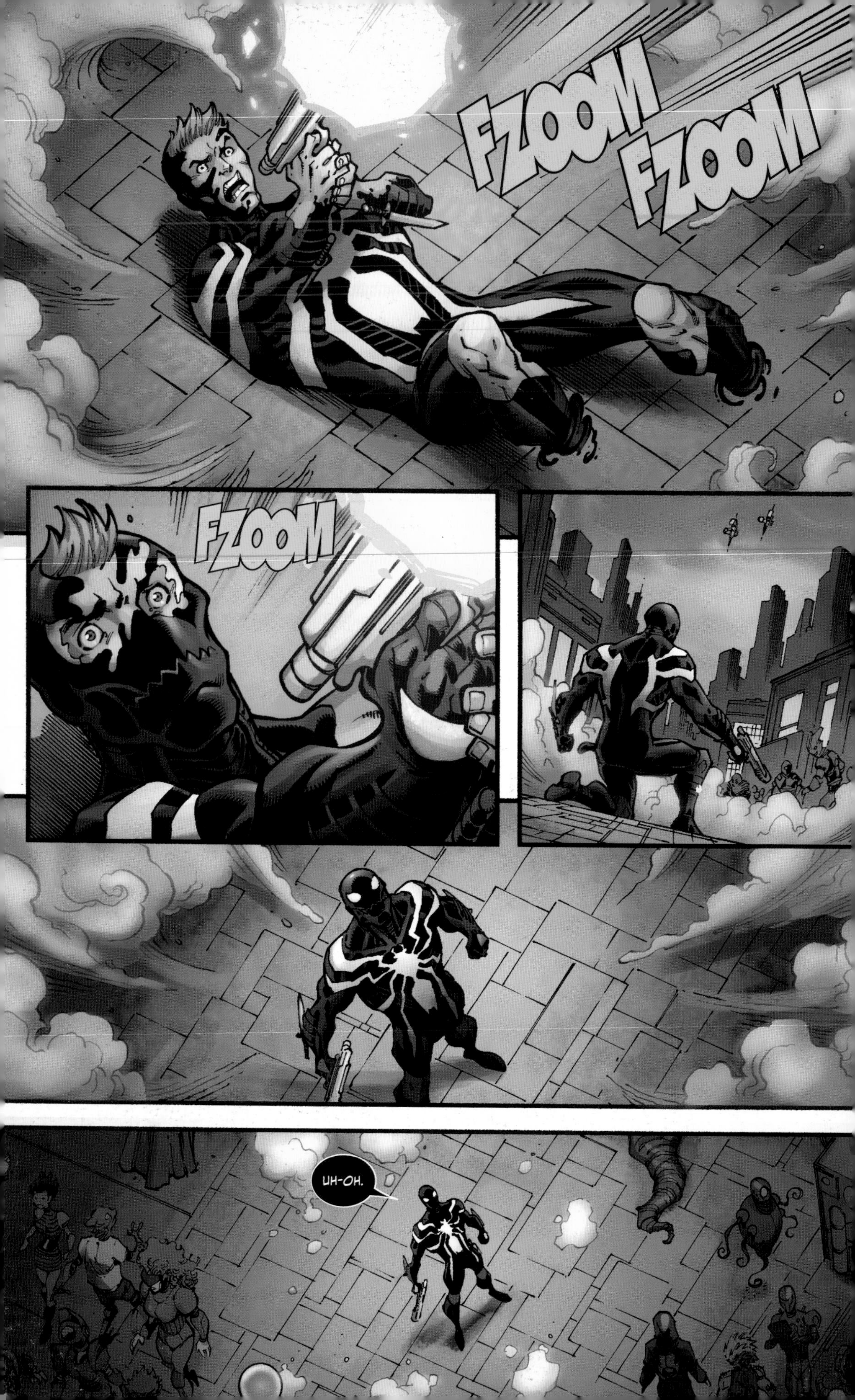
FZOOM
FZOOM
FZOOM
UH-OH.

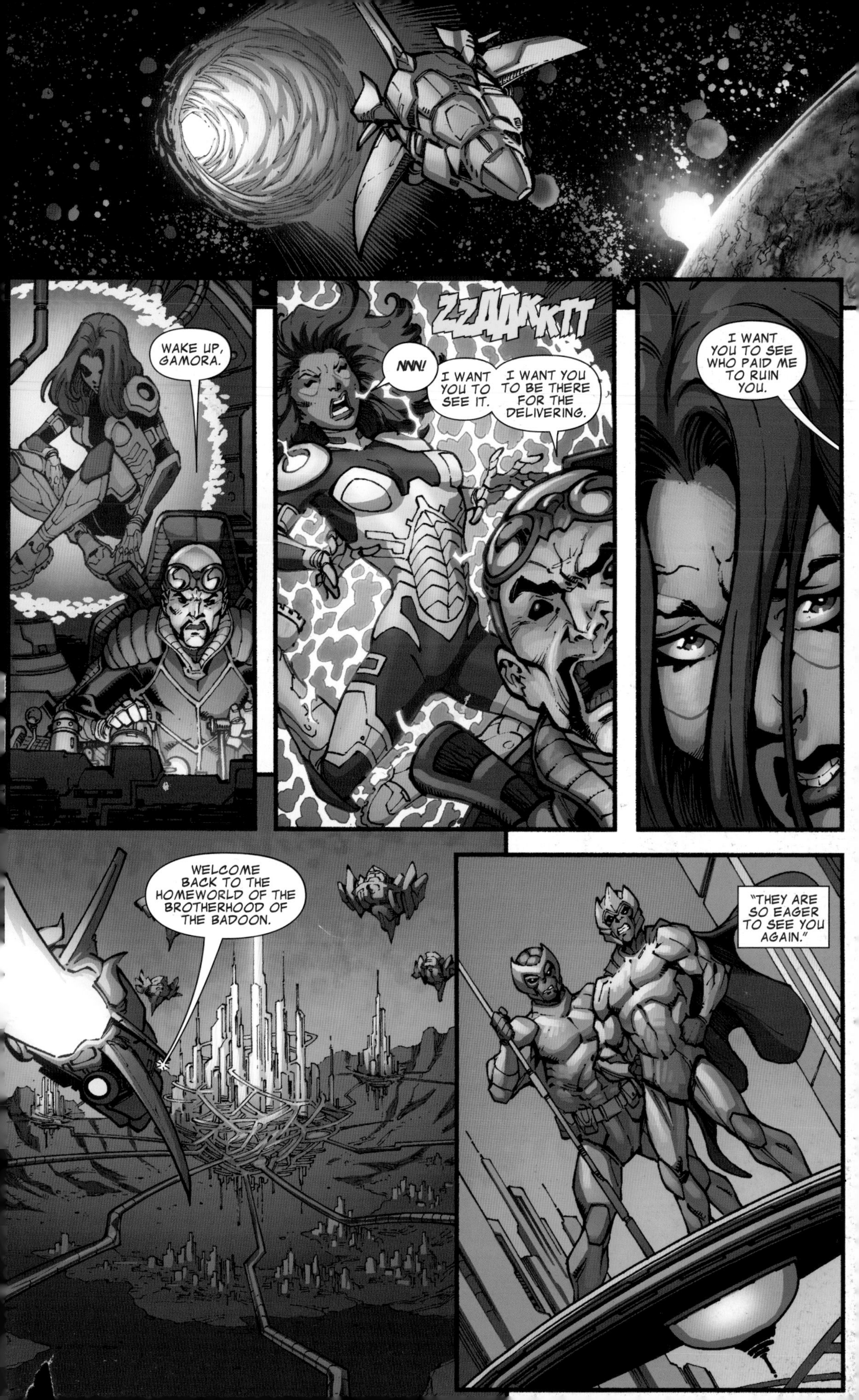
WAKE UP, GAMORA.
ZZAAKKKTT
NNN!
I WANT YOU TO SEE IT.
I WANT YOU TO BE THERE FOR THE DELIVERING.
I WANT YOU TO SEE WHO PAID ME TO RUIN YOU.
WELCOME BACK TO THE HOMEWORLD OF THE BROTHERHOOD OF THE BADOON.
"THEY ARE SO EAGER TO SEE YOU AGAIN."

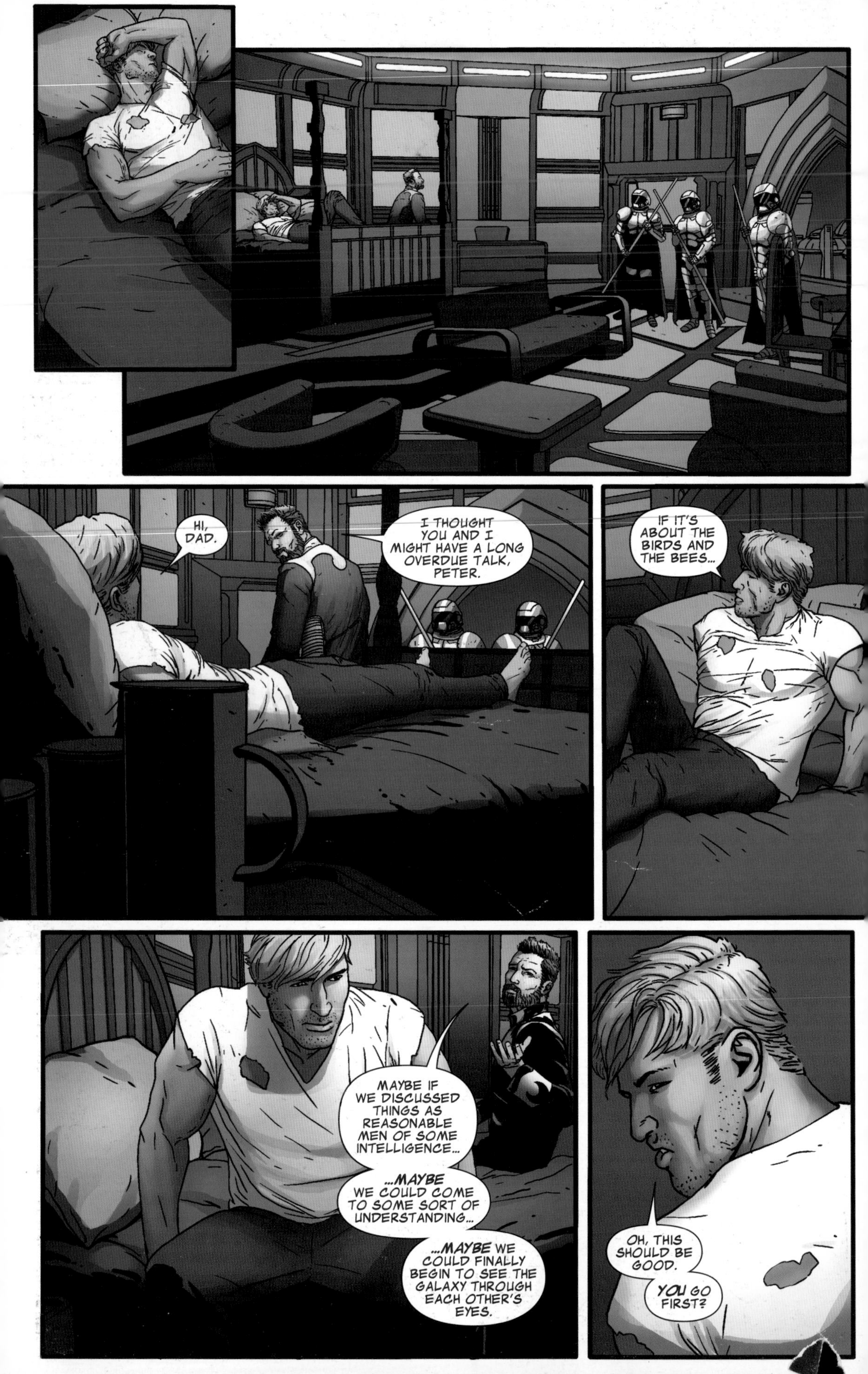
HI, DAD.
I THOUGHT YOU AND I MIGHT HAVE A LONG OVERDUE TALK, PETER.
IF IT'S ABOUT THE BIRDS AND THE BEES...
MAYBE IF WE DISCUSSED THINGS AS REASONABLE MEN OF SOME INTELLIGENCE...
...MAYBE WE COULD COME TO SOME SORT OF UNDERSTANDING...
...MAYBE WE COULD FINALLY BEGIN TO SEE THE GALAXY THROUGH EACH OTHER'S EYES.
OH, THIS SHOULD BE GOOD.
YOU GO FIRST?

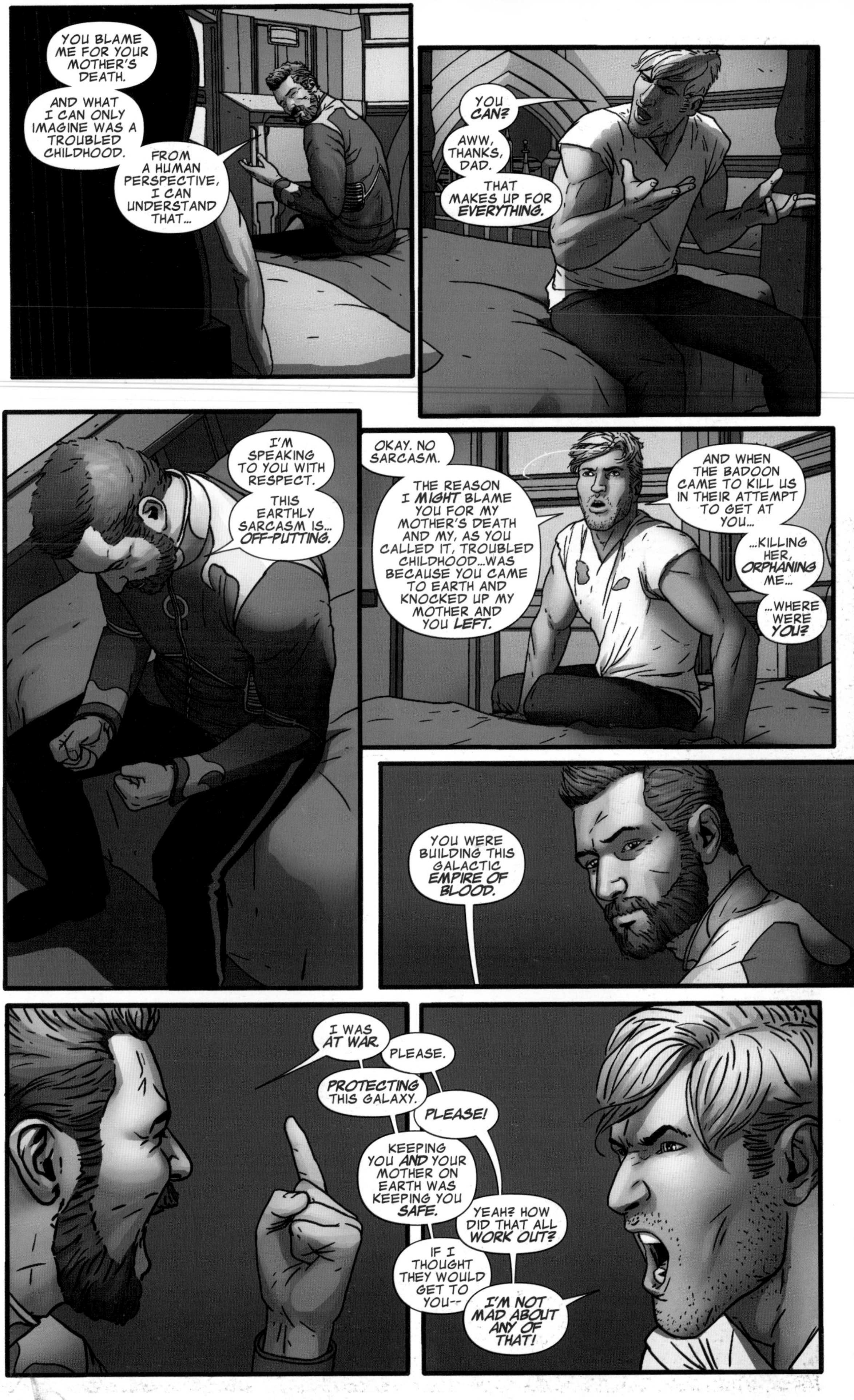
YOU BLAME ME FOR YOUR MOTHER'S DEATH.
AND WHAT I CAN ONLY IMAGINE WAS A TROUBLED CHILDHOOD.
FROM A HUMAN PERSPECTIVE, I CAN UNDERSTAND THAT...
YOU CAN?
AWW, THANKS, DAD.
THAT MAKES UP FOR EVERYTHING.
I'M SPEAKING TO YOU WITH RESPECT.
THIS EARTHLY SARCASM IS... OFF-PUTTING.
OKAY. NO SARCASM.
THE REASON I MIGHT BLAME YOU FOR MY MOTHER'S DEATH AND MY, AS YOU CALLED IT, TROUBLED CHILDHOOD...WAS BECAUSE YOU CAME TO EARTH AND KNOCKED UP MY MOTHER AND YOU LEFT.
AND WHEN THE BADOON CAME TO KILL US IN THEIR ATTEMPT TO GET AT YOU...
...KILLING HER, ORPHANING ME...
...WHERE WERE YOU?
YOU WERE BUILDING THIS GALACTIC EMPIRE OF BLOOD.
I WAS AT WAR.
PLEASE.
PROTECTING THIS GALAXY.
PLEASE!
KEEPING YOU AND YOUR MOTHER ON EARTH WAS KEEPING YOU SAFE.
YEAH? HOW DID THAT ALL WORK OUT?
IF I THOUGHT THEY WOULD GET TO YOU--
I'M NOT MAD ABOUT ANY OF THAT!

I'M MAD THAT I GREW UP TO DISCOVER YOU'RE A *CONNIVING WARLORD* WHO THINKS THE GALAXY SHOULD ANSWER TO HIM AND *ONLY* HIM.

I THINK THIS GALAXY SHOULD BE FREE TO THINK AND CREATE AND DO WHATEVER IT IS THEY NEED TO DO TO FEEL ALIVE WITHOUT WORRYING WHAT *YOU'RE* GOING TO DO ABOUT IT.

YOU CONQUER. YOU'RE A WARLORD.

IT *DISGUSTS* ME.

I LEAD BECAUSE IT IS THE NATURE OF THINGS.

IF NOT ME, IT WOULD BE *THANOS.*

IF NOT ME, THE *SKRULLS* WOULD RUN AMOK.

IF NOT ME, THE *BADOON* WOULD--

STOP.

YOU COULD SO EASILY BE HERE, BY MY SIDE, EMBRACING ALL OF THE GOOD FORTUNE OUR POSITION IN THIS LIFE HAS TO OFFER.

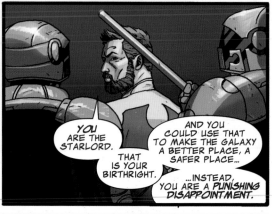

YOU ARE THE STARLORD. THAT IS YOUR BIRTHRIGHT.

AND YOU COULD USE THAT TO MAKE THE GALAXY A BETTER PLACE, A SAFER PLACE...

...INSTEAD, YOU ARE A *PUNISHING* DISAPPOINTMENT.

RIGHT BACK AT YA, DAD.

SO YOU UNDERSTAND YOUR SITUATION...

...THE GUARDIANS OF THE GALAXY ARE *NO MORE.*

THEY HAVE BEEN DEALT WITH INDIVIDUALLY.

YOUR MANY ENEMIES HAVE EACH BEEN REWARDED WITH THE CAPTURE OF ONE OF YOUR "TEAM."

IT WAS THE ONLY LOGICAL OUTCOME TO YOUR RAMBUNCTIOUS AND CARELESS BEHAVIOR.

WHAT DO YOU MEAN, YOU DEALT WITH--?

YOU WILL BE DEALT WITH HERE ACCORDING TO THE LAWS.

WITH NO SPECIAL COURTESY OR FAVOR.

YOU ARE AN *ENEMY OF THE EMPIRE,* PETER QUILL...

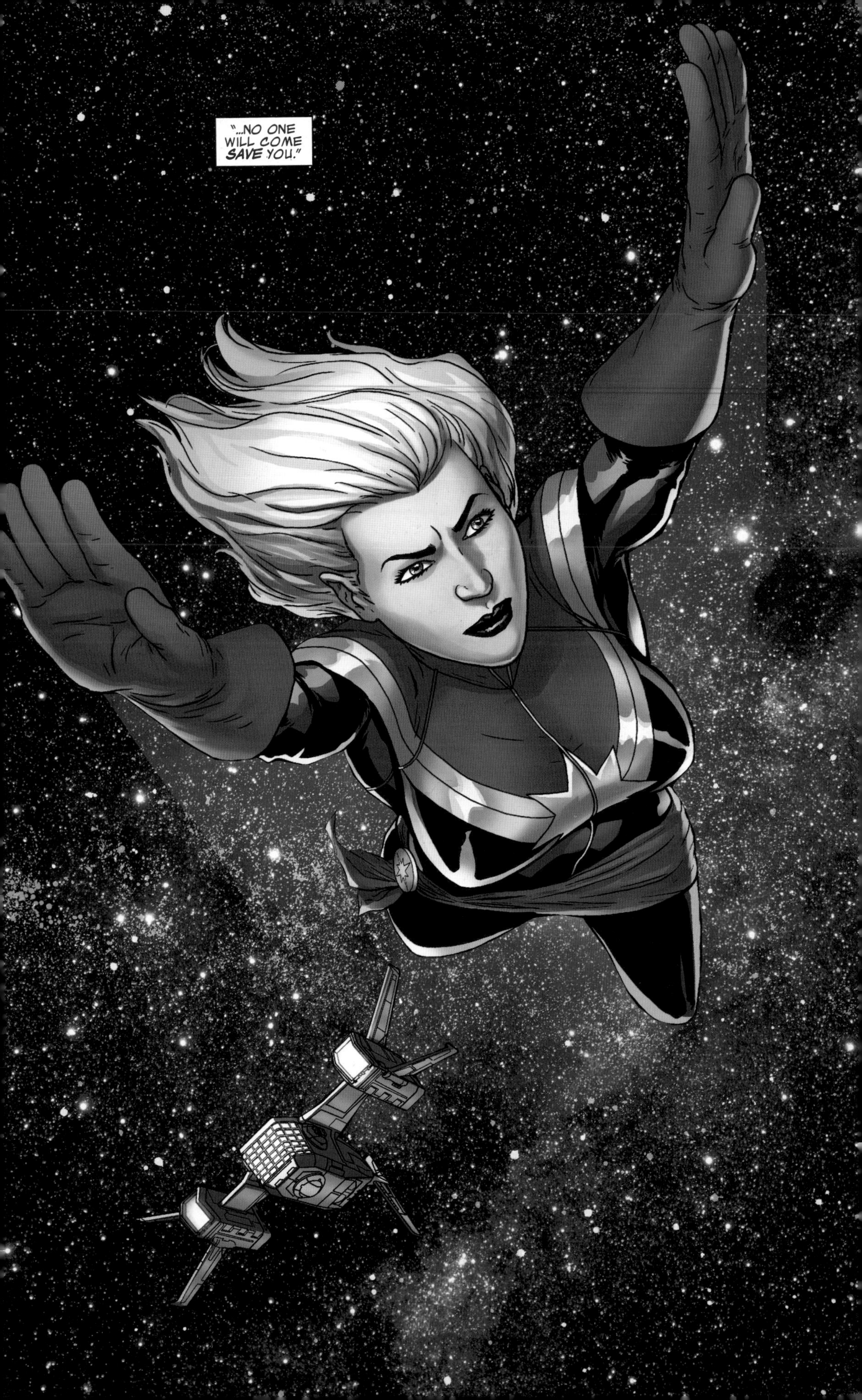
"...NO ONE WILL COME SAVE YOU."

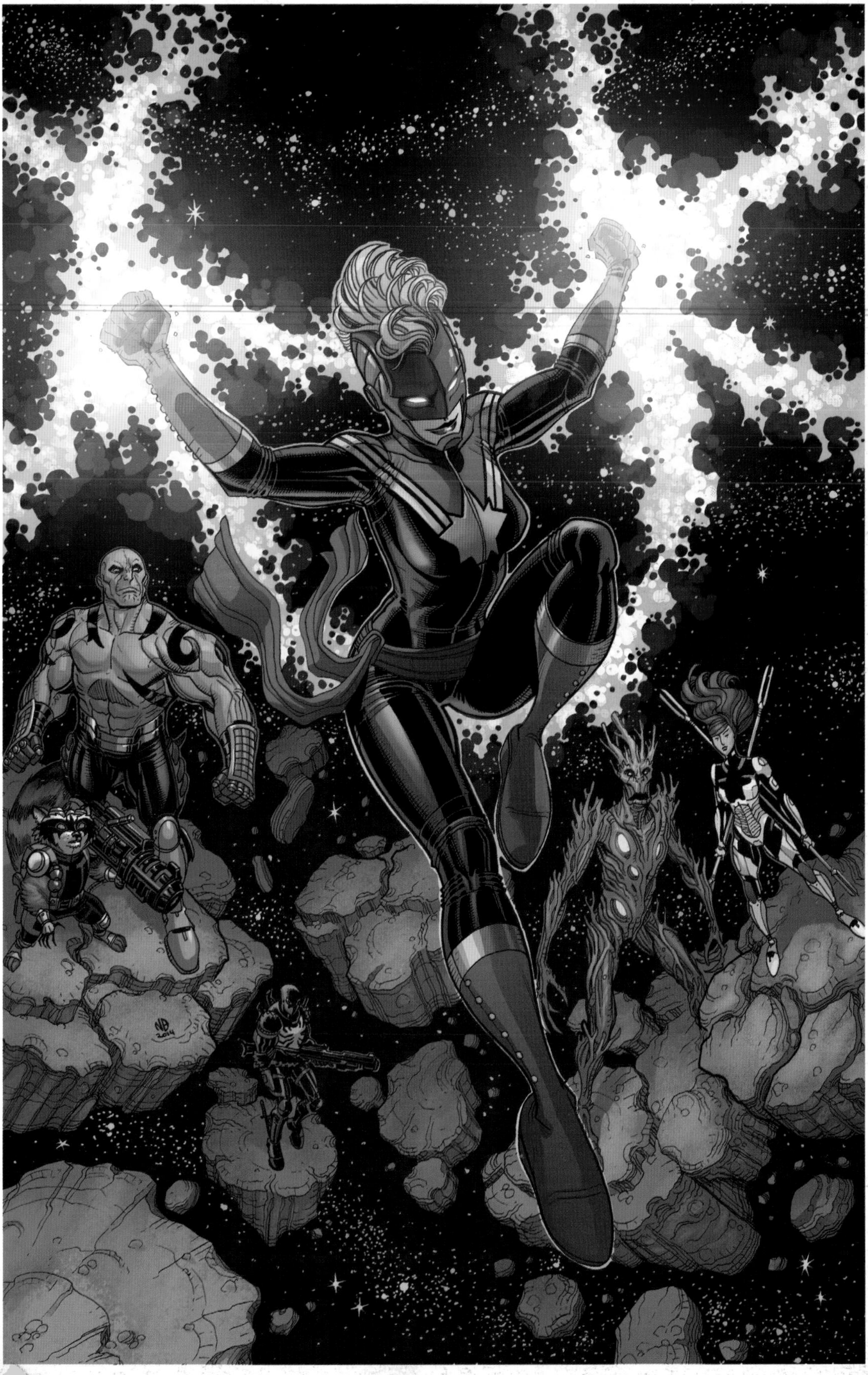

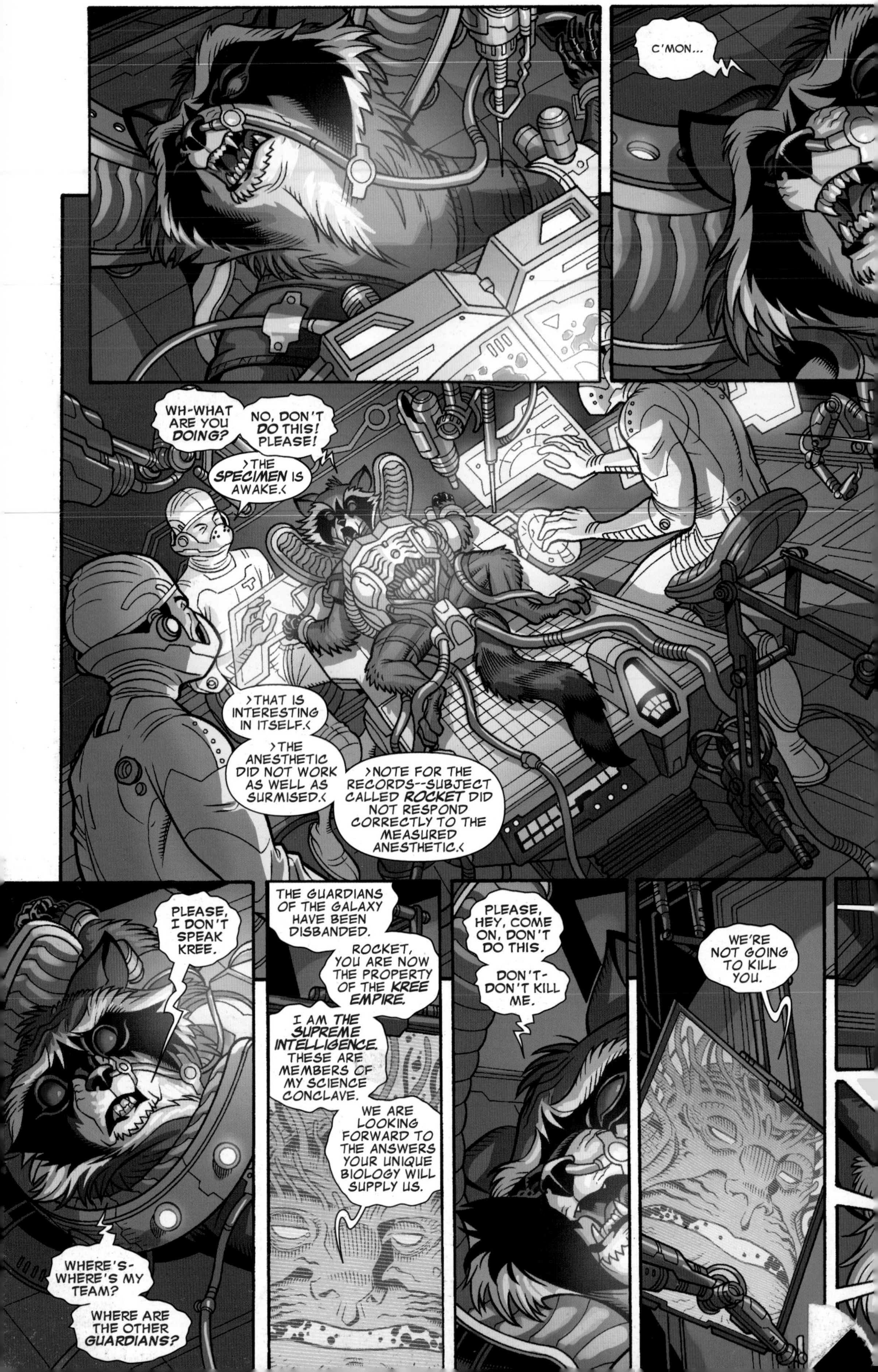
C'MON...
WH-WHAT ARE YOU *DOING?*
NO, DON'T *DO* THIS! PLEASE!
›THE *SPECIMEN* IS AWAKE.‹
›THAT IS INTERESTING IN ITSELF.‹
›THE ANESTHETIC DID NOT WORK AS WELL AS SURMISED.‹
›NOTE FOR THE RECORDS--SUBJECT CALLED *ROCKET* DID NOT RESPOND CORRECTLY TO THE MEASURED ANESTHETIC.‹
PLEASE, I DON'T SPEAK KREE.
WHERE'S- WHERE'S MY TEAM?
WHERE ARE THE OTHER *GUARDIANS?*
THE GUARDIANS OF THE GALAXY HAVE BEEN DISBANDED.
ROCKET, YOU ARE NOW THE PROPERTY OF THE *KREE EMPIRE.*
I AM *THE SUPREME INTELLIGENCE.* THESE ARE MEMBERS OF MY SCIENCE CONCLAVE.
WE ARE LOOKING FORWARD TO THE ANSWERS YOUR UNIQUE BIOLOGY WILL SUPPLY US.
PLEASE, HEY, COME ON, DON'T DO THIS.
DON'T- DON'T KILL ME.
WE'RE NOT GOING TO KILL YOU.

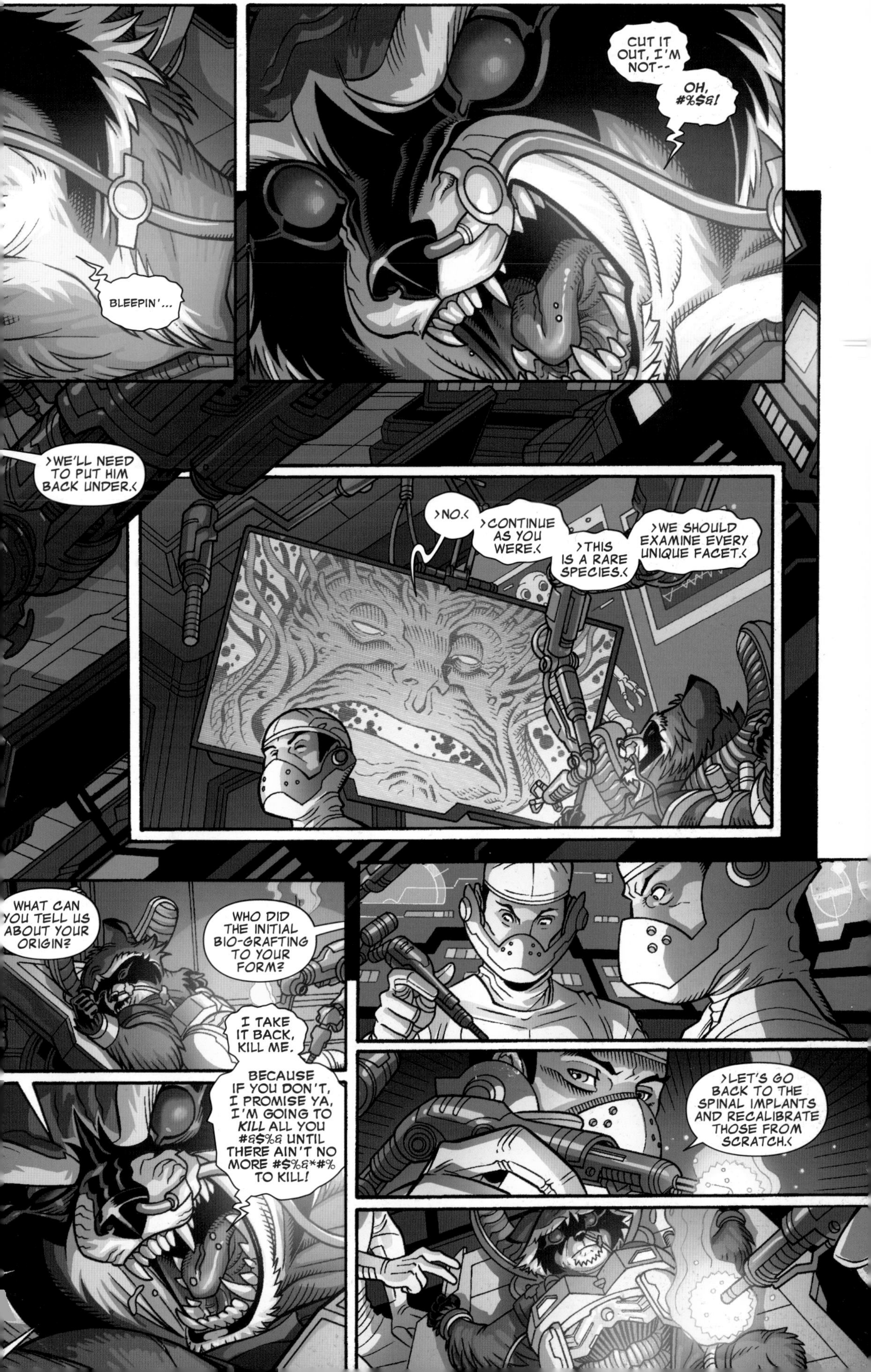
BLEEPIN'...
CUT IT OUT, I'M NOT--
OH, #%$&!
>WE'LL NEED TO PUT HIM BACK UNDER.<
>NO.<
>CONTINUE AS YOU WERE.<
>THIS IS A RARE SPECIES.<
>WE SHOULD EXAMINE EVERY UNIQUE FACET.<
WHAT CAN YOU TELL US ABOUT YOUR ORIGIN?
WHO DID THE INITIAL BIO-GRAFTING TO YOUR FORM?
I TAKE IT BACK, KILL ME.
BECAUSE IF YOU DON'T, I PROMISE YA, I'M GOING TO KILL ALL YOU #&$%& UNTIL THERE AIN'T NO MORE #$%&*#% TO KILL!
>LET'S GO BACK TO THE SPINAL IMPLANTS AND RECALIBRATE THOSE FROM SCRATCH.<

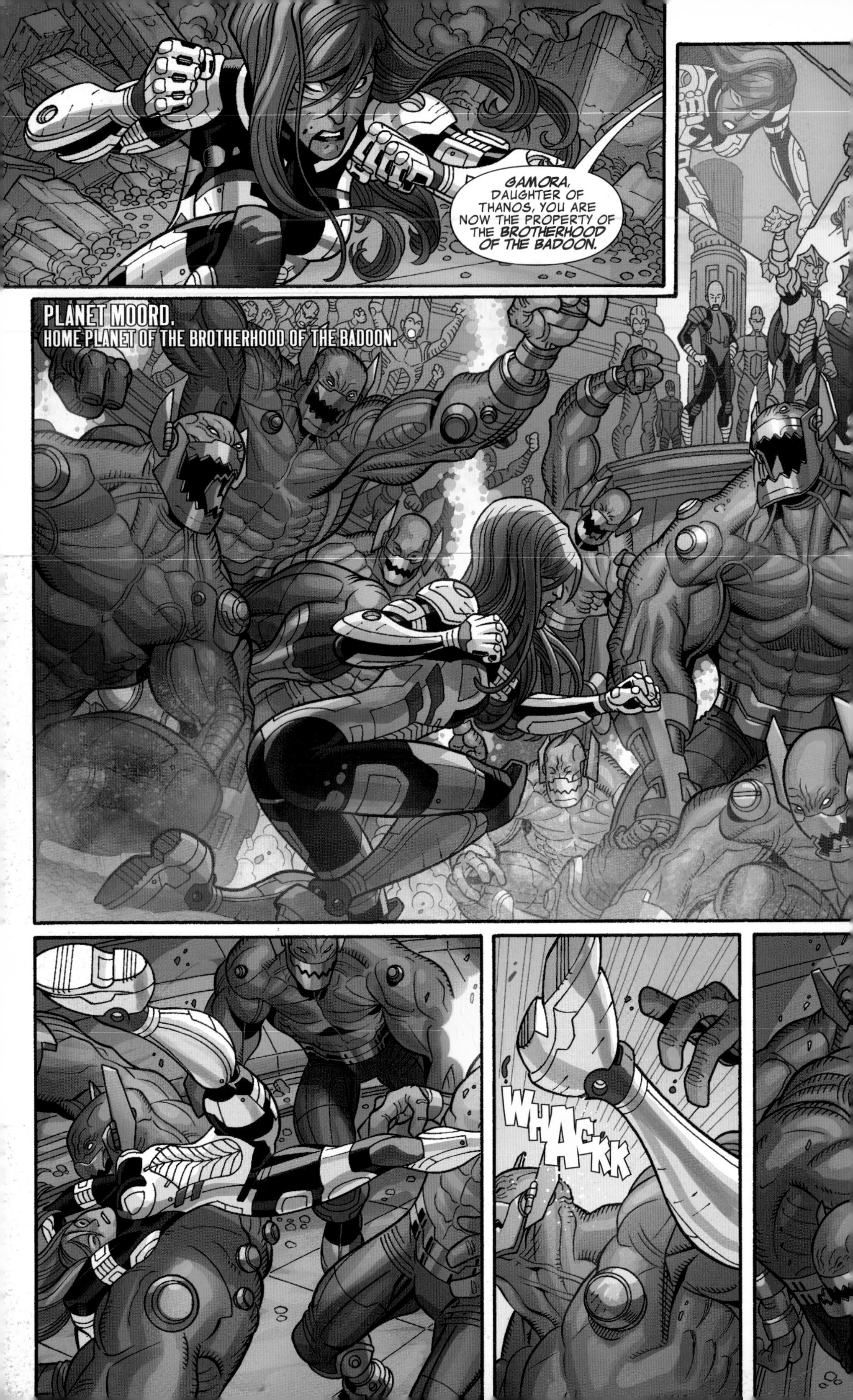
GAMORA, DAUGHTER OF THANOS, YOU ARE NOW THE PROPERTY OF THE BROTHERHOOD OF THE BADOON.
PLANET MOORD.
HOME PLANET OF THE BROTHERHOOD OF THE BADOON.
WHACKK

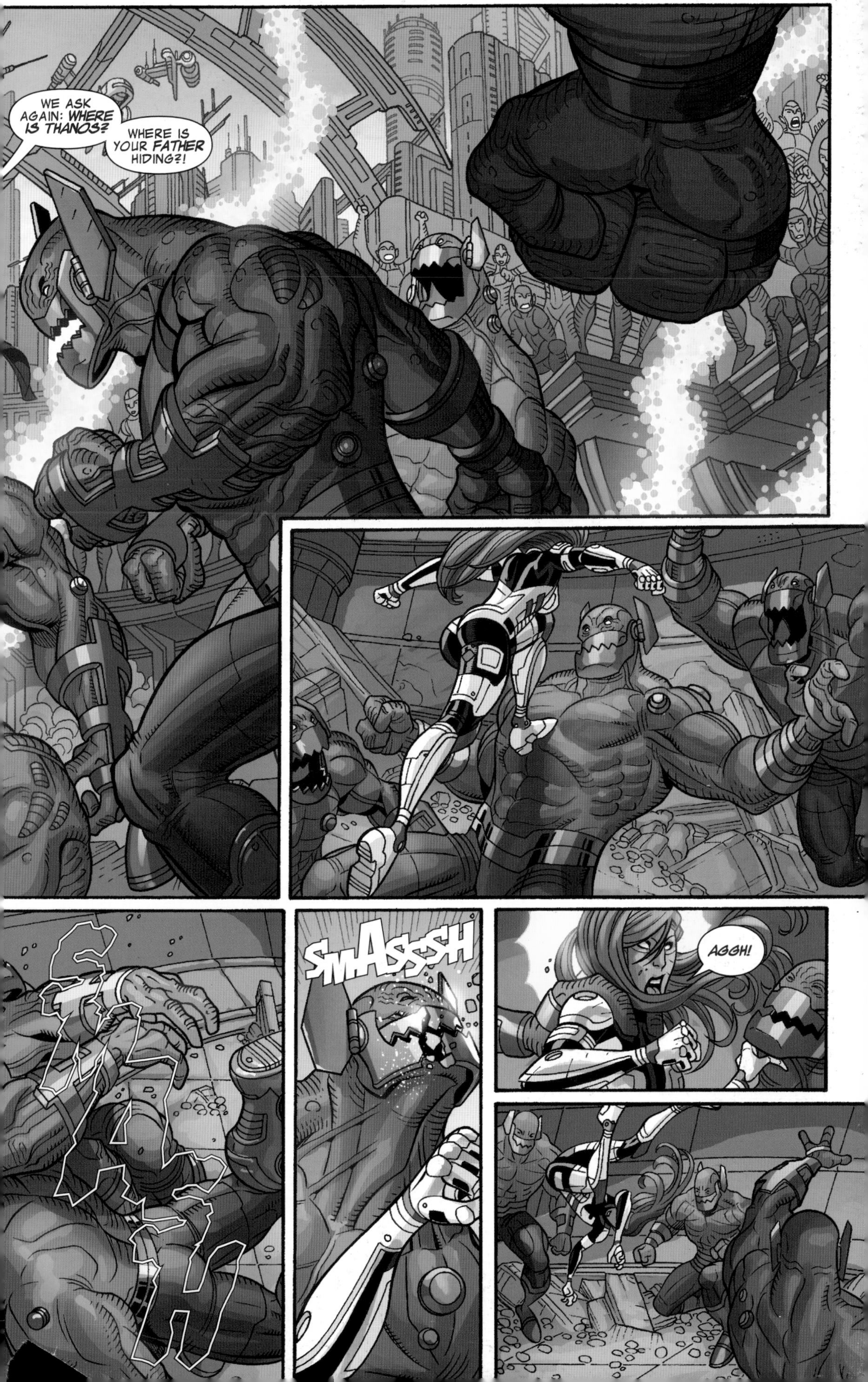
WE ASK AGAIN: WHERE IS THANOS?
WHERE IS YOUR FATHER HIDING?!
SMASSSH
AGGH!

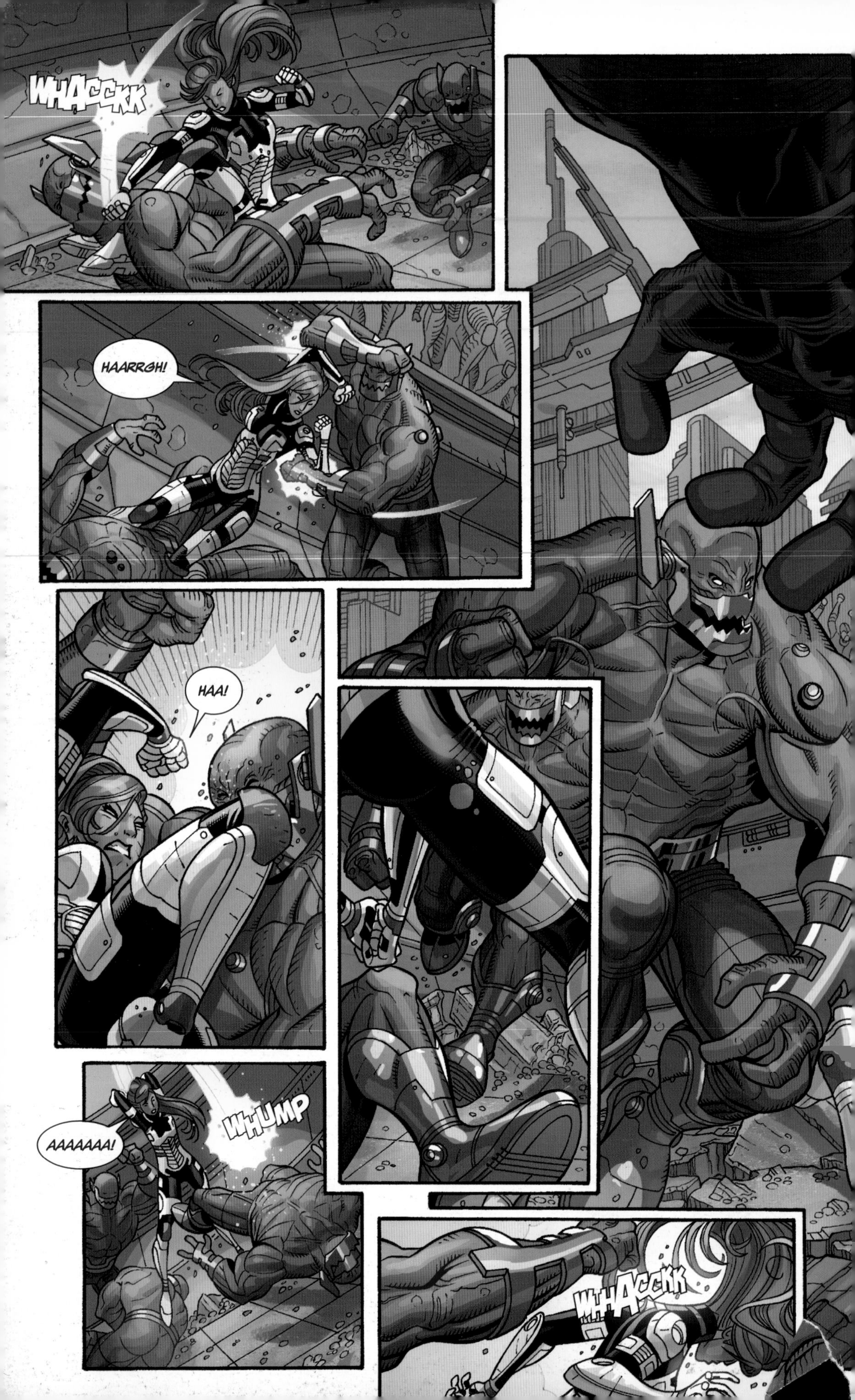
WHACCKK
HAARRGH!
HAA!
AAAAAAA!
WHUMP
WHACCKK

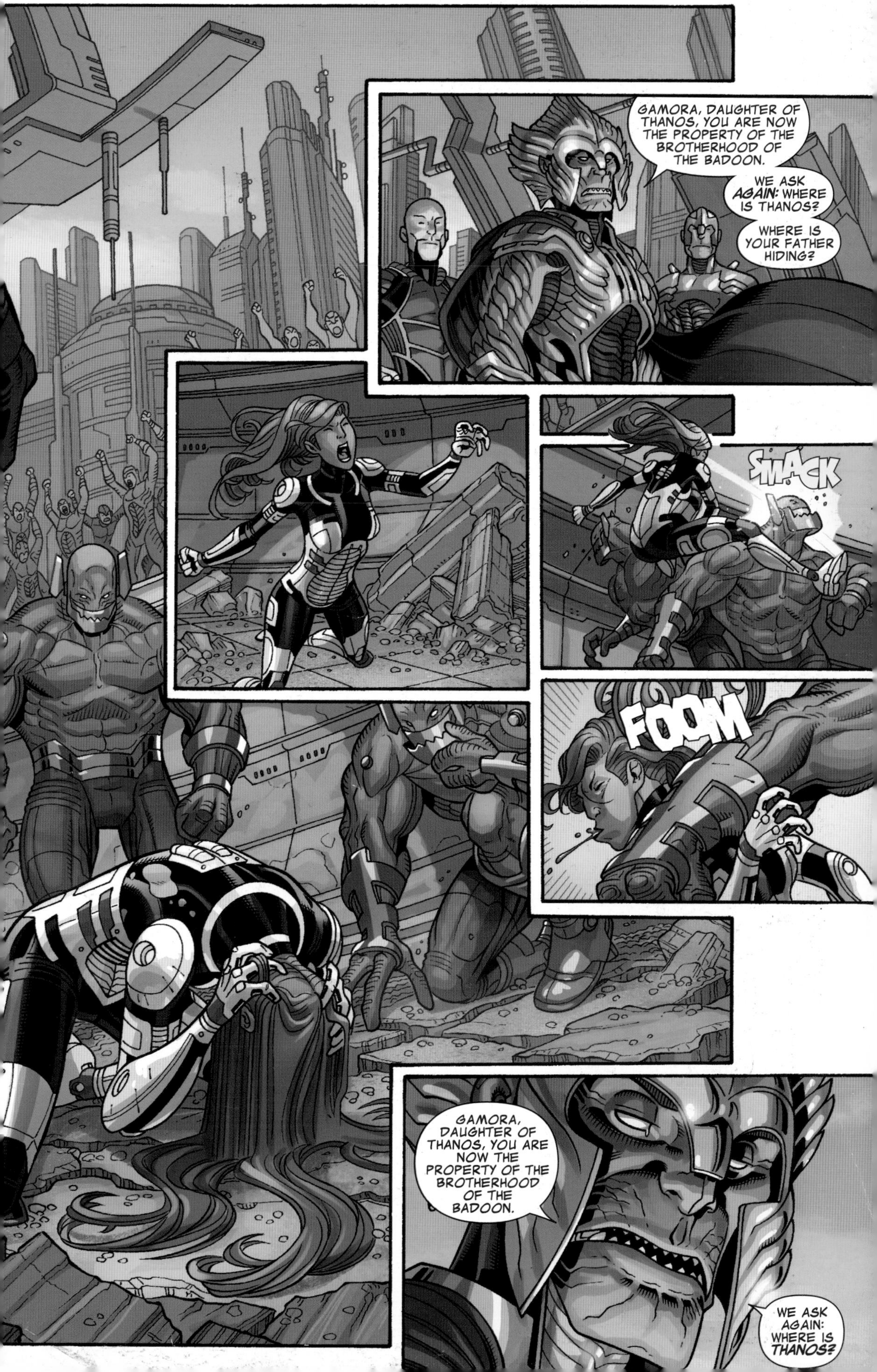
GAMORA, DAUGHTER OF THANOS, YOU ARE NOW THE PROPERTY OF THE BROTHERHOOD OF THE BADOON.
WE ASK AGAIN: WHERE IS THANOS?
WHERE IS YOUR FATHER HIDING?
SMACK
FOOM
GAMORA, DAUGHTER OF THANOS, YOU ARE NOW THE PROPERTY OF THE BROTHERHOOD OF THE BADOON.
WE ASK AGAIN: WHERE IS THANOS?

I AM **MANTA** OF THE SHI'AR IMPERIAL GUARD.

I SPEAK NOW FOR THE LEADER AND CHOSEN PRAETOR, GLADIATOR.

ARTHUR SAMPSON DOUGLAS, A.K.A. **DRAX THE DESTROYER,** YOU ARE NOW A PRISONER OF THE SHI'AR EMPIRE.

YOU WILL ANSWER FOR YOUR CRIMES AGAINST THE GALAXY.

YOU WILL ANSWER FOR YOUR NUMEROUS COUNTS OF PIRACY, MURDER, CONSPIRACY...

THAT IS NOT AN APPROPRIATE RESPONSE TO YOUR SITUATION.

YOU ARE A COWARD.

YOU ARE TO BE HELD UNTIL A PROPER TRIAL IS SCHEDULED FOR YOU.

THIS IS ILL-THOUGHT-OUT RETALIATION FOR THE GUARDIANS STOPPING YOUR ILL-THOUGHT-OUT SCHEME TO PUNISH THE EARTH FOR YOUR FAILINGS AS A LEADER.

THE GUARDIANS ARE **NO MORE.**

YOU WILL BE **PUNISHED** FOR YOUR CRIMES

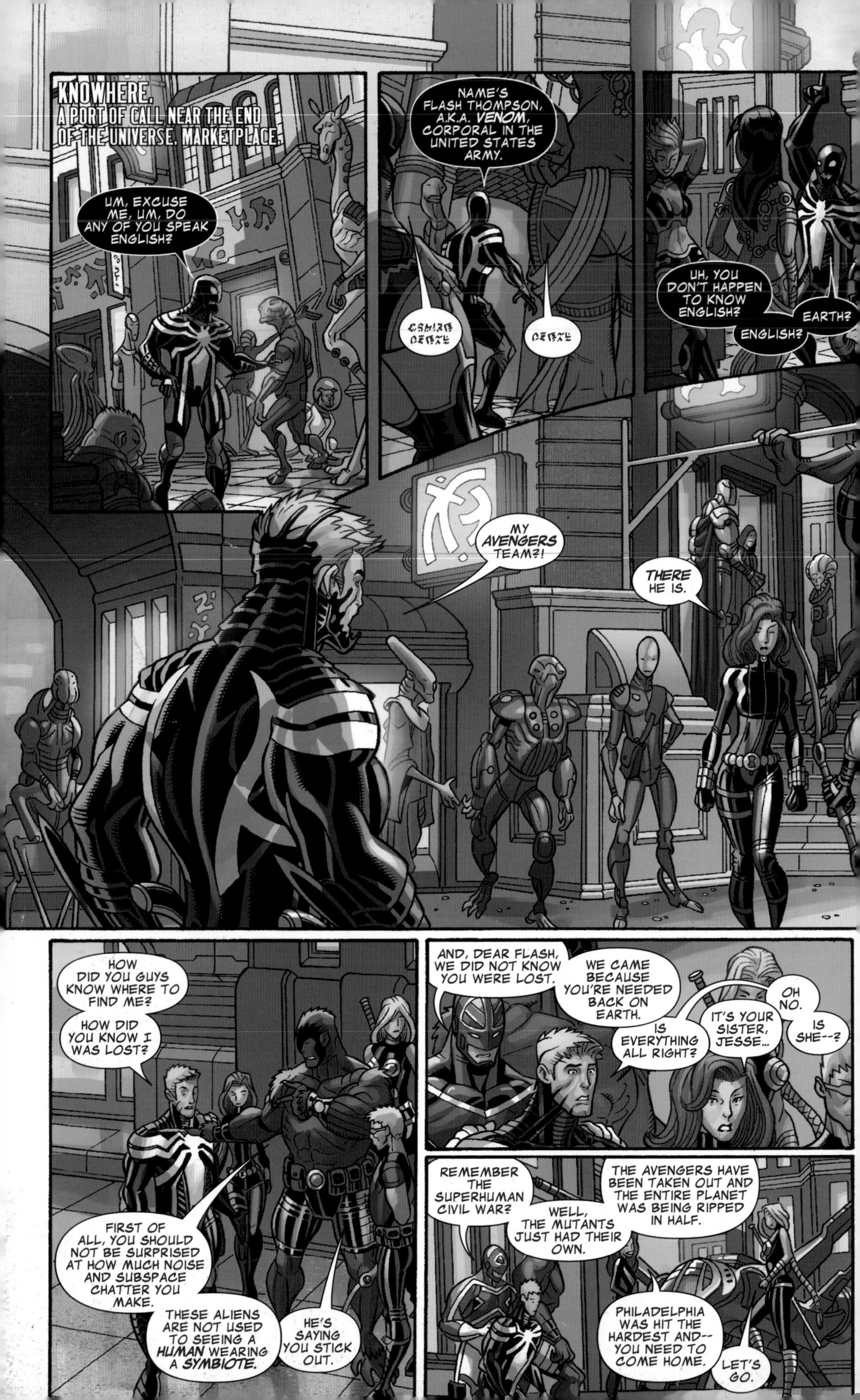
KNOWHERE.
A PORT OF CALL NEAR THE END OF THE UNIVERSE. MARKETPLACE.
UM, EXCUSE ME, UM, DO ANY OF YOU SPEAK ENGLISH?
NAME'S FLASH THOMPSON, A.K.A. VENOM, CORPORAL IN THE UNITED STATES ARMY.
UH, YOU DON'T HAPPEN TO KNOW ENGLISH?
EARTH?
ENGLISH?
MY AVENGERS TEAM?!
THERE HE IS.
HOW DID YOU GUYS KNOW WHERE TO FIND ME?
HOW DID YOU KNOW I WAS LOST?
FIRST OF ALL, YOU SHOULD NOT BE SURPRISED AT HOW MUCH NOISE AND SUBSPACE CHATTER YOU MAKE.
THESE ALIENS ARE NOT USED TO SEEING A HUMAN WEARING A SYMBIOTE.
HE'S SAYING YOU STICK OUT.
AND, DEAR FLASH, WE DID NOT KNOW YOU WERE LOST.
WE CAME BECAUSE YOU'RE NEEDED BACK ON EARTH.
IS EVERYTHING ALL RIGHT?
IT'S YOUR SISTER, JESSE...
OH NO.
IS SHE--?
REMEMBER THE SUPERHUMAN CIVIL WAR?
WELL, THE MUTANTS JUST HAD THEIR OWN.
THE AVENGERS HAVE BEEN TAKEN OUT AND THE ENTIRE PLANET WAS BEING RIPPED IN HALF.
PHILADELPHIA WAS HIT THE HARDEST AND-- YOU NEED TO COME HOME.
LET'S GO.

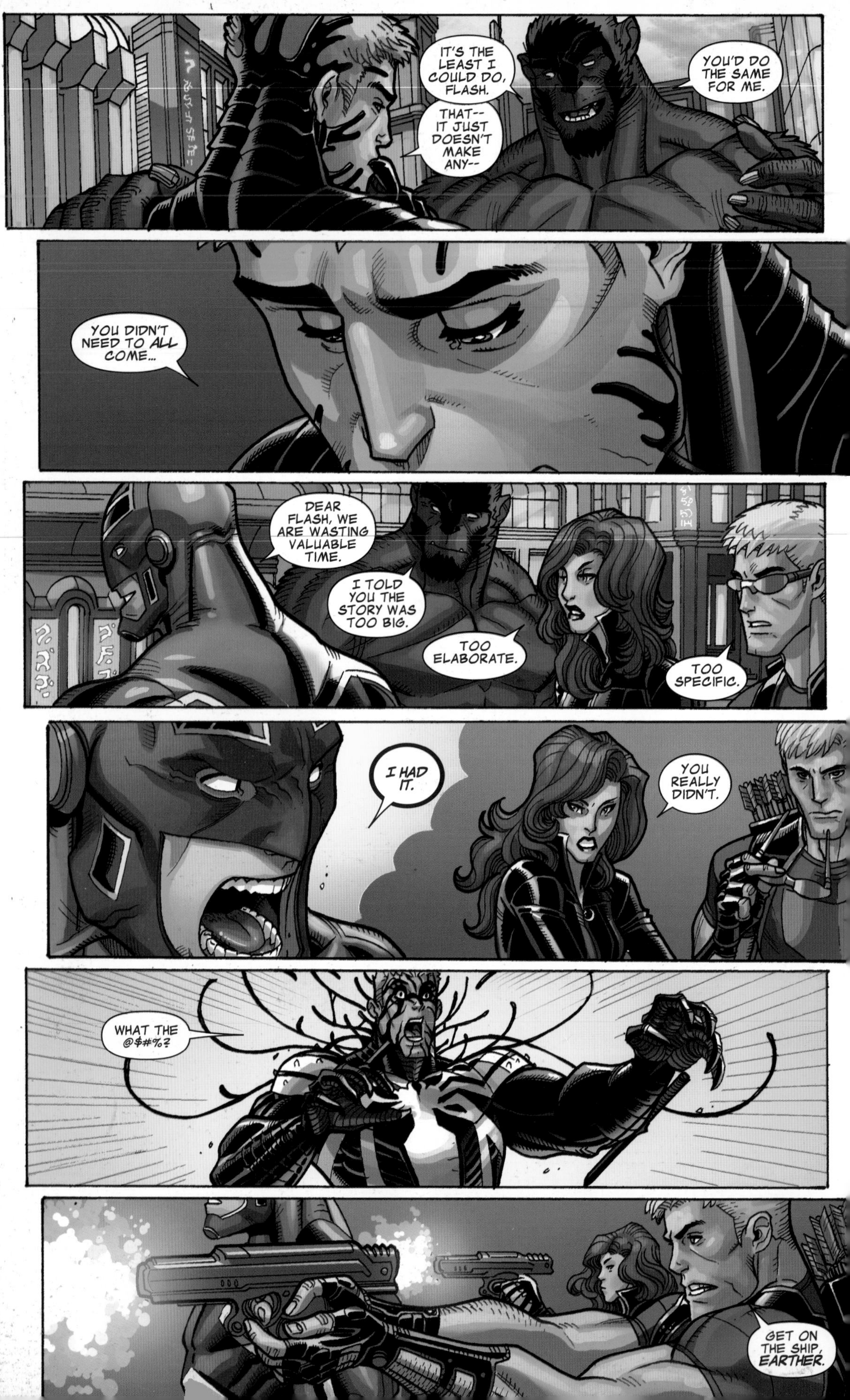
IT'S THE LEAST I COULD DO, FLASH.
THAT-- IT JUST DOESN'T MAKE ANY--
YOU'D DO THE SAME FOR ME.
YOU DIDN'T NEED TO ALL COME...
DEAR FLASH, WE ARE WASTING VALUABLE TIME.
I TOLD YOU THE STORY WAS TOO BIG.
TOO ELABORATE.
TOO SPECIFIC.
I HAD IT.
YOU REALLY DIDN'T.
WHAT THE @$#%?
GET ON THE SHIP, EARTHER.

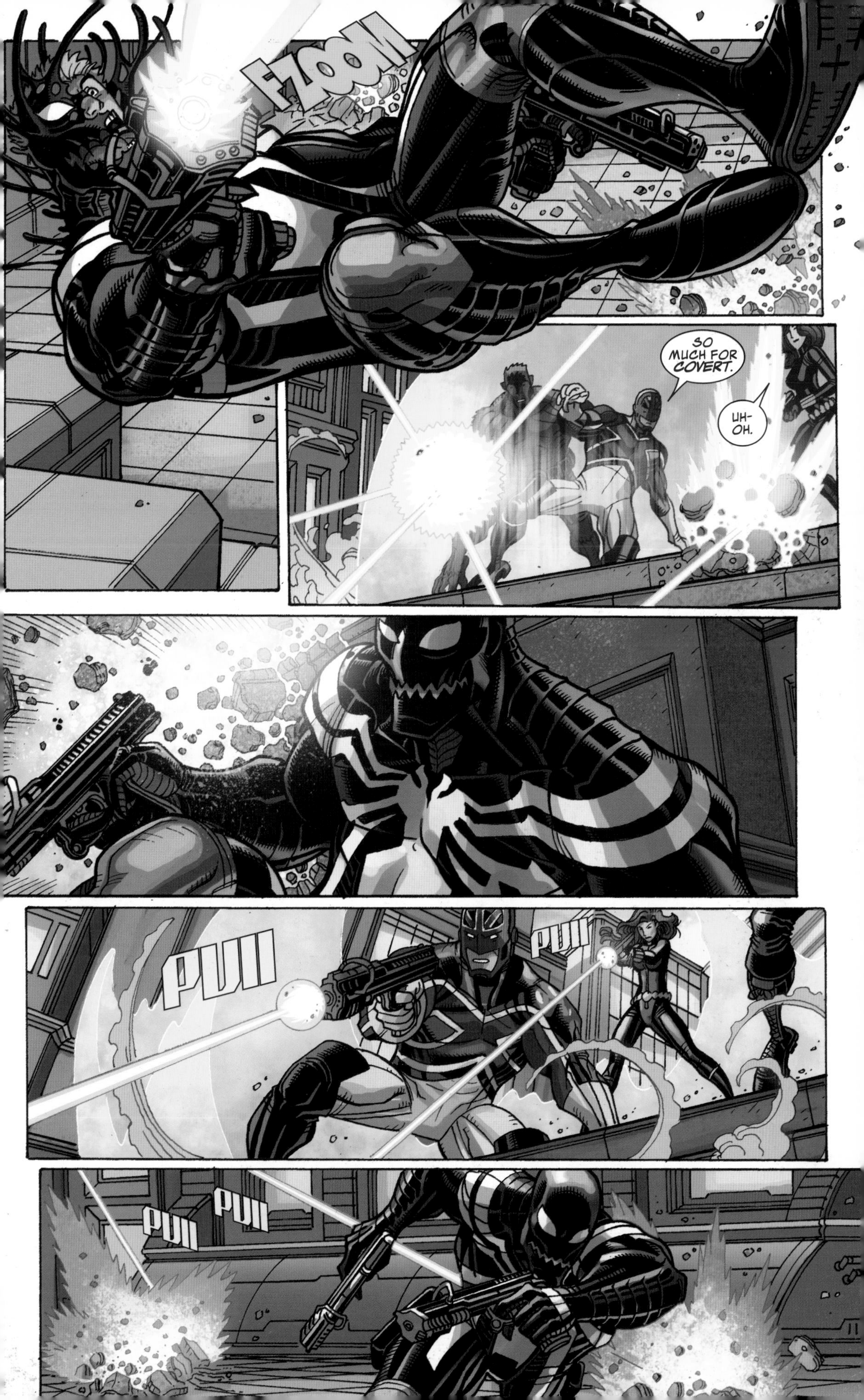
FZOOM
SO MUCH FOR COVERT.
UH-OH.
PUII
PUII
PUII
PUII

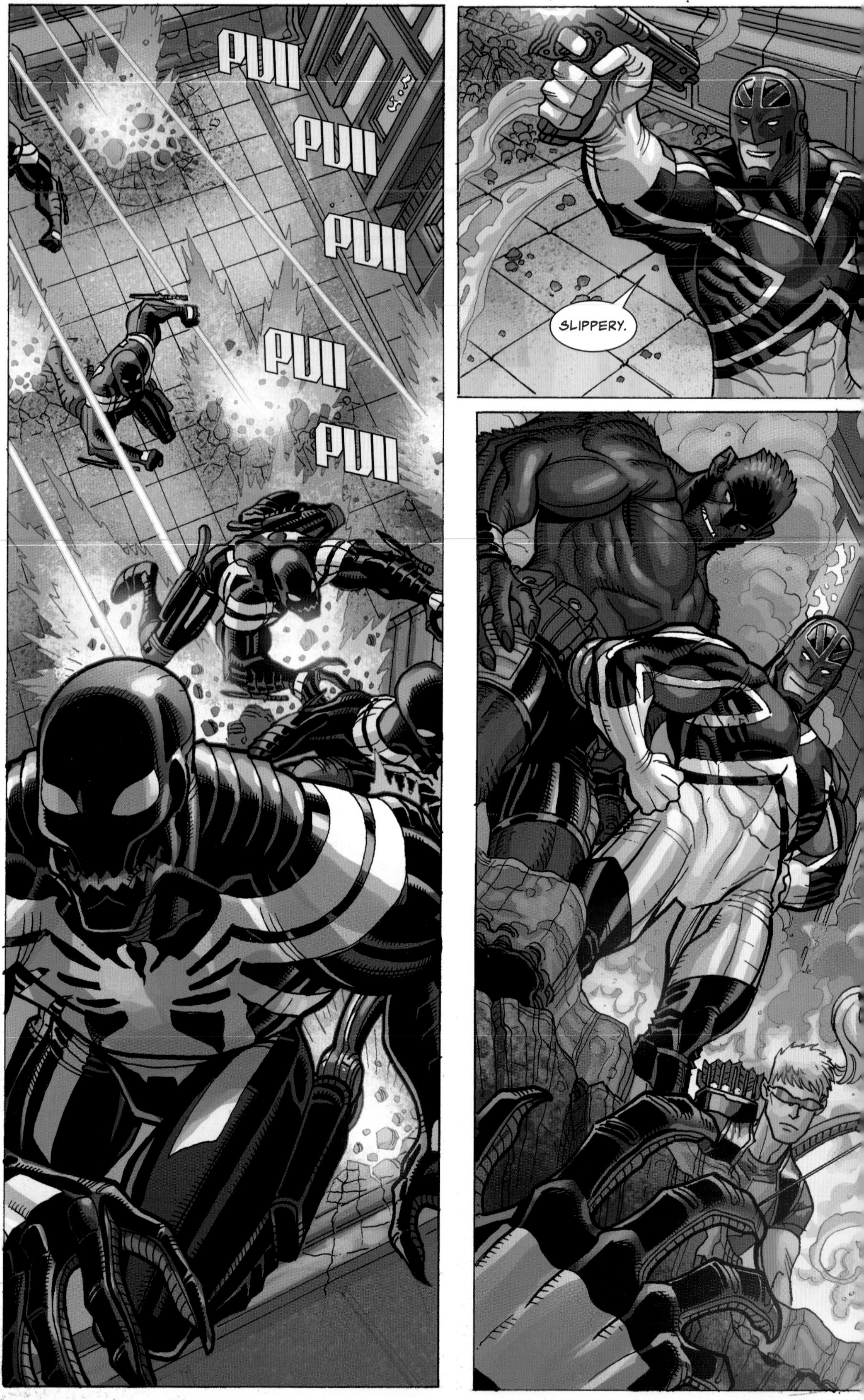
PUII
PUII
PUII
PUII
PUII
SLIPPERY.

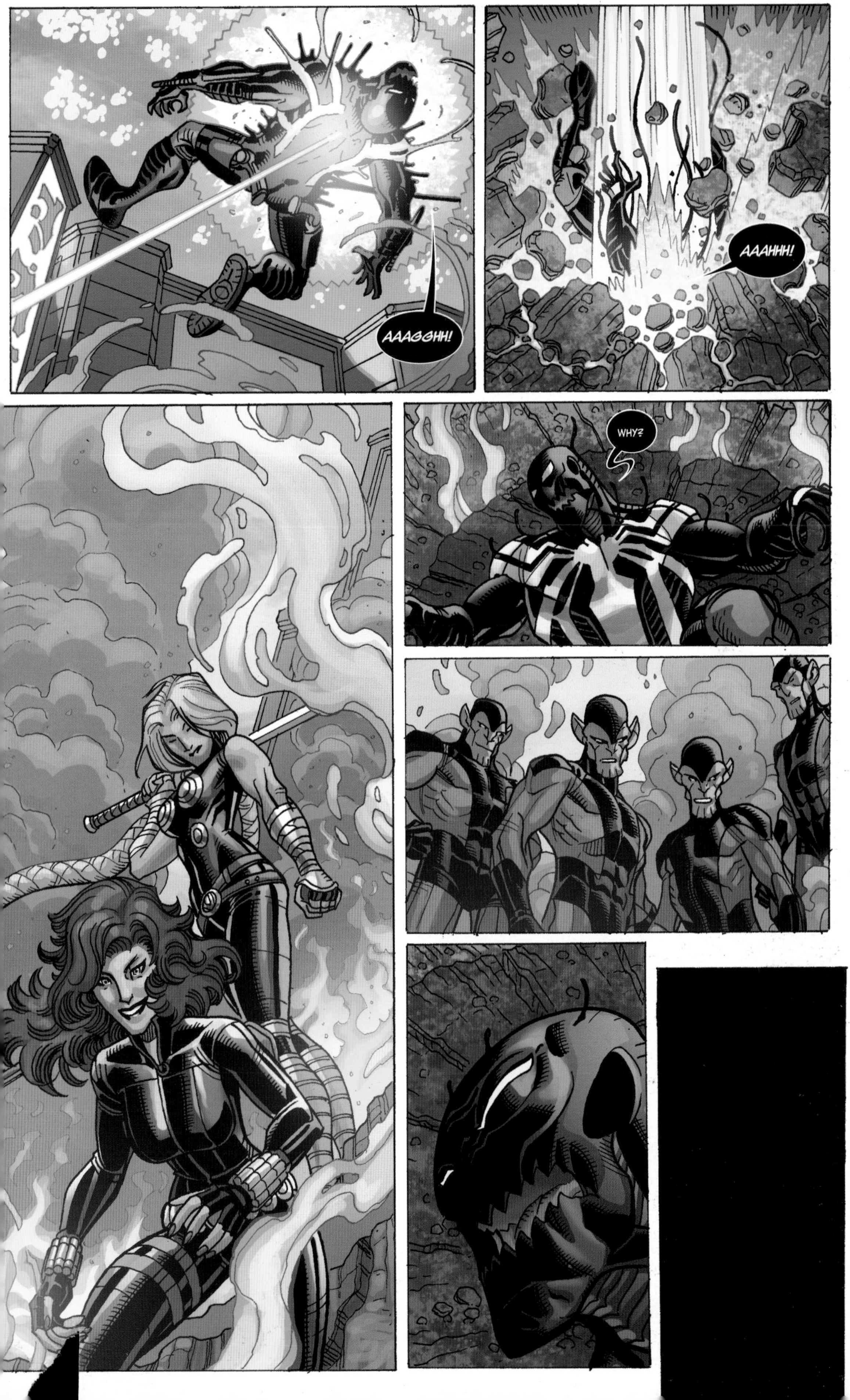
AAAGGHH!
AAAHHH!
WHY?

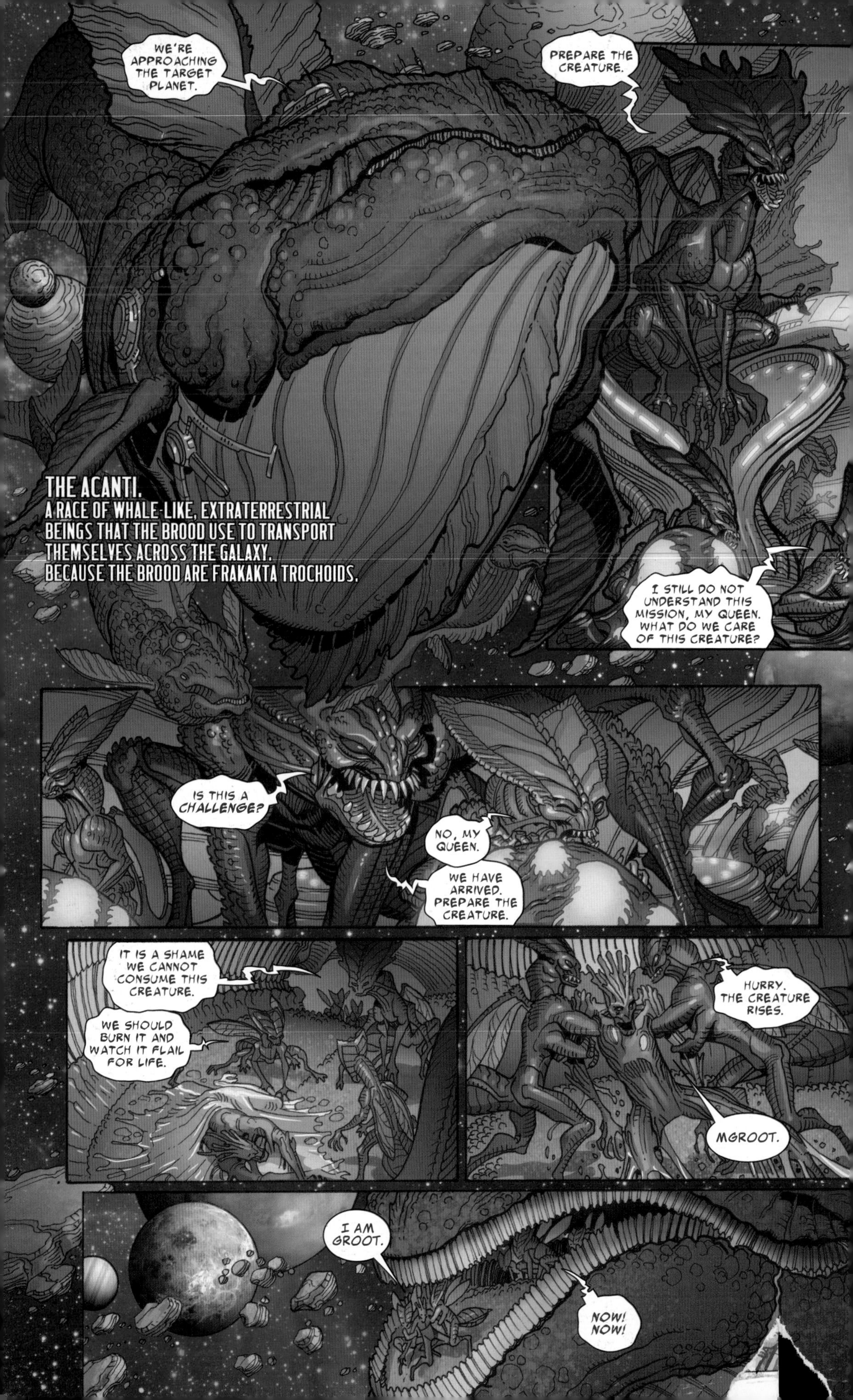
WE'RE APPROACHING THE TARGET PLANET.
PREPARE THE CREATURE.
THE ACANTI.
A RACE OF WHALE-LIKE, EXTRATERRESTRIAL BEINGS THAT THE BROOD USE TO TRANSPORT THEMSELVES ACROSS THE GALAXY.
BECAUSE THE BROOD ARE FRAKAKTA TROCHOIDS.
I STILL DO NOT UNDERSTAND THIS MISSION, MY QUEEN. WHAT DO WE CARE OF THIS CREATURE?
IS THIS A CHALLENGE?
NO, MY QUEEN.
WE HAVE ARRIVED. PREPARE THE CREATURE.
IT IS A SHAME WE CANNOT CONSUME THIS CREATURE.
WE SHOULD BURN IT AND WATCH IT FLAIL FOR LIFE.
HURRY. THE CREATURE RISES.
MGROOT.
I AM GROOT.
NOW! NOW!

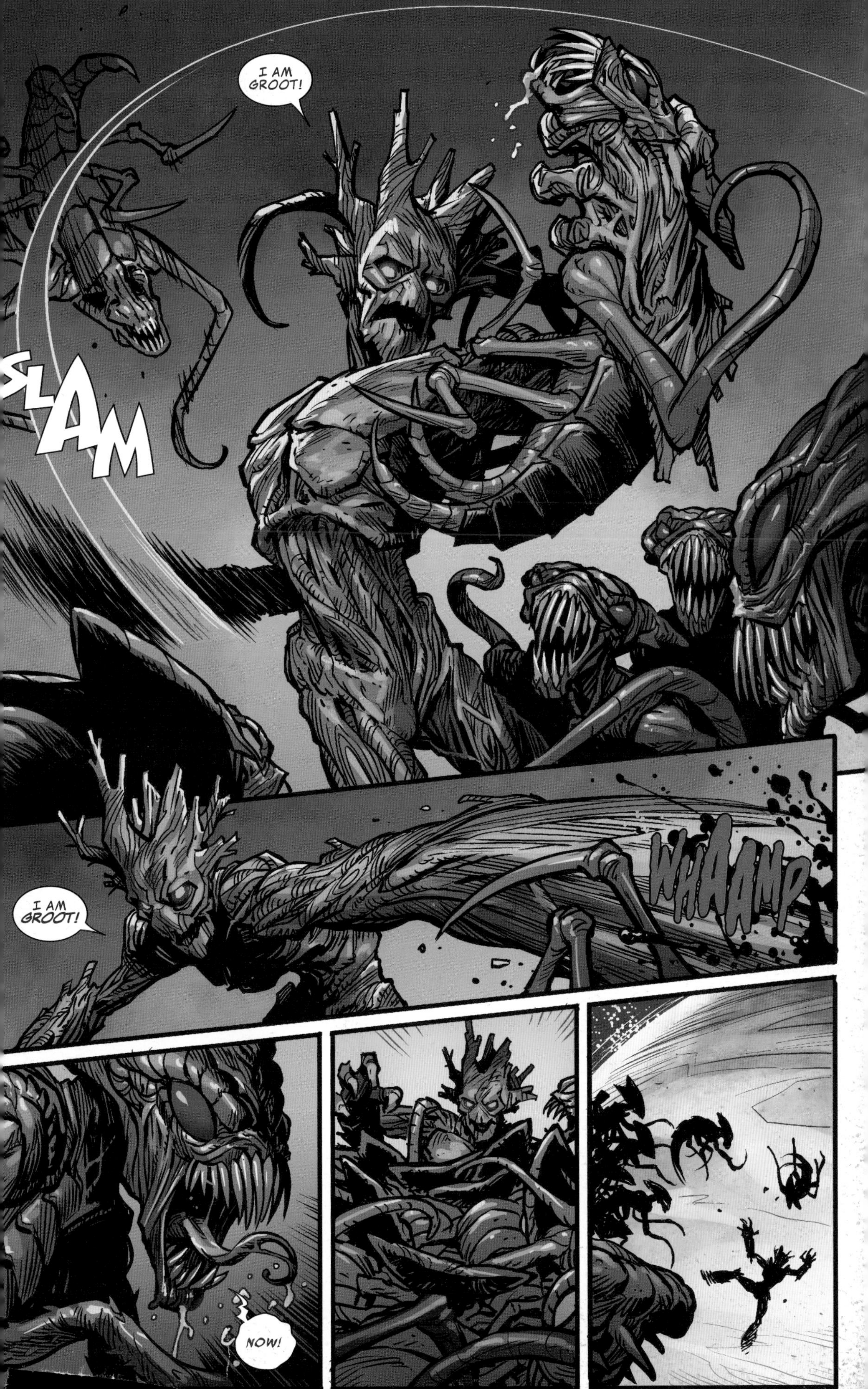
I AM GROOT!
SLAM
WHAAAMP
I AM GROOT!
NOW!

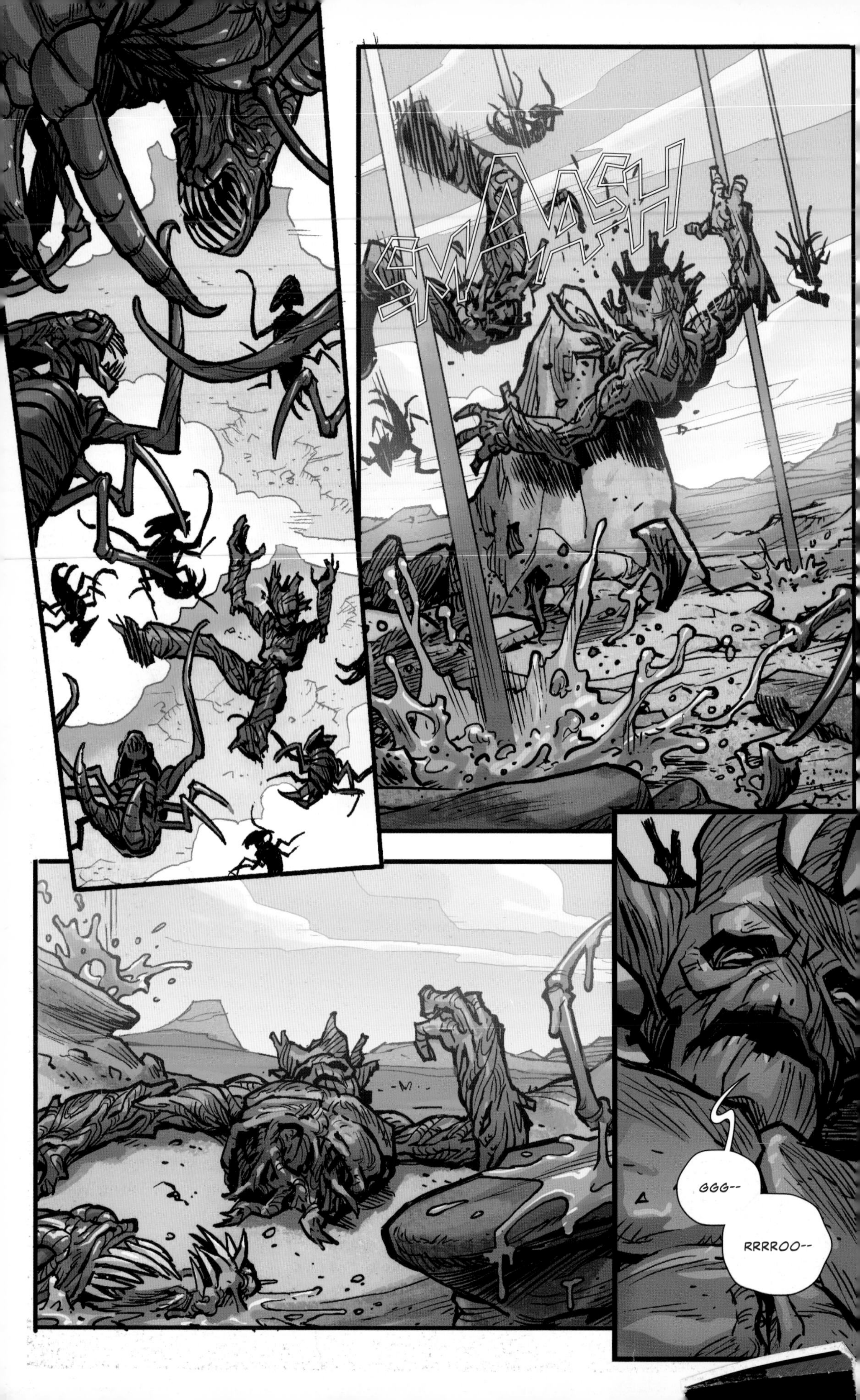
SWASH
GGG--
RRRROO--

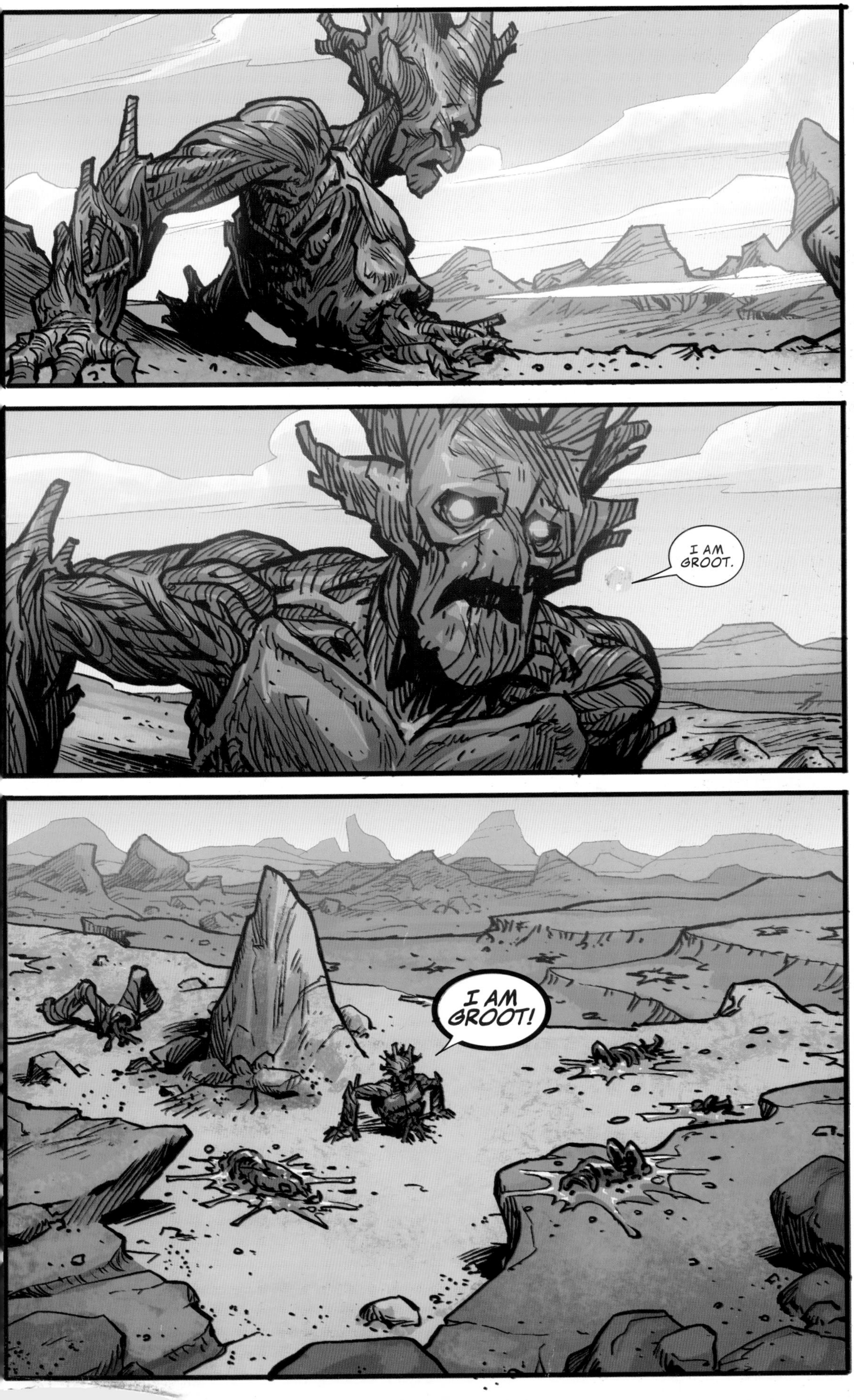
I AM GROOT.
I AM GROOT!

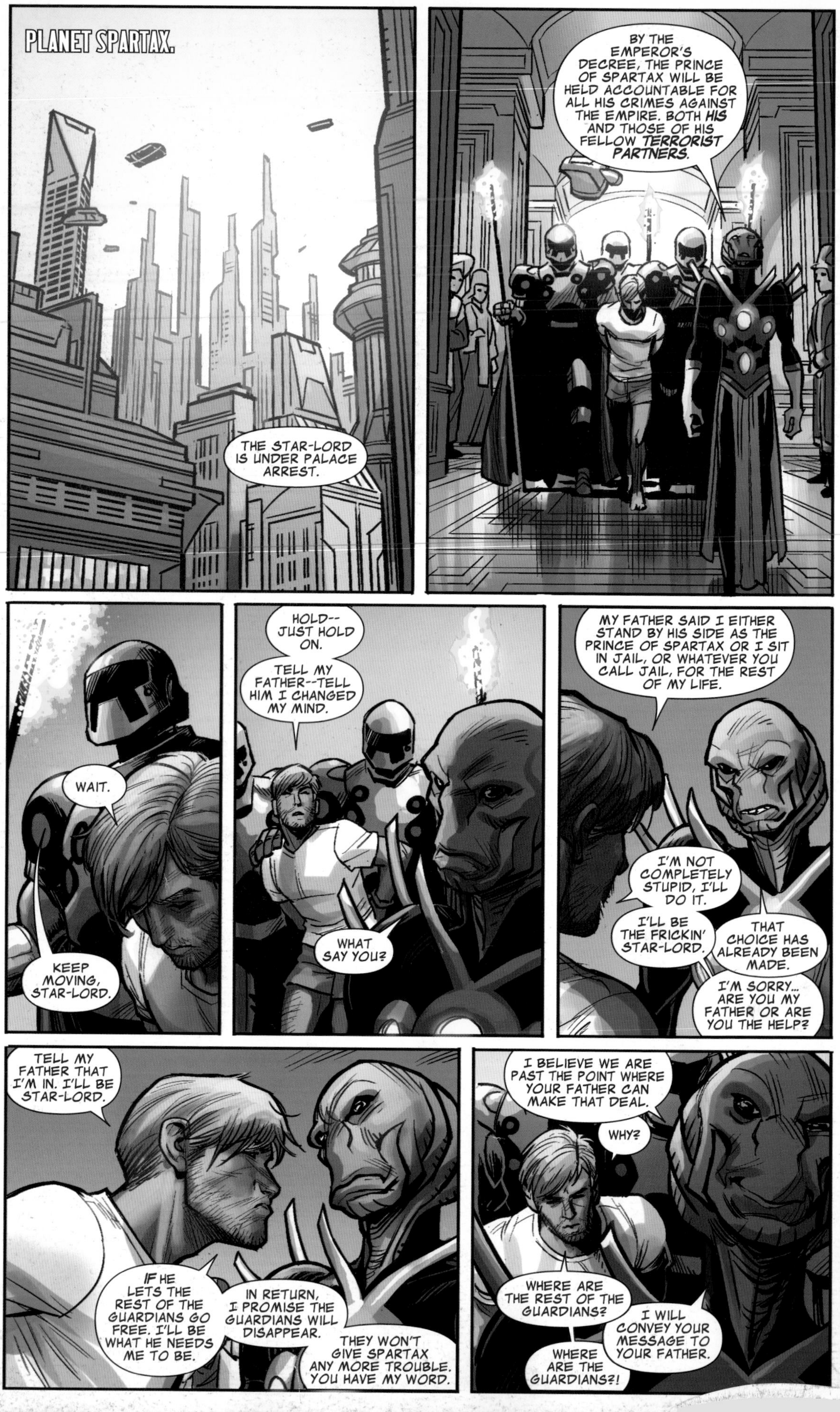
PLANET SPARTAX.
THE STAR-LORD IS UNDER PALACE ARREST.
BY THE EMPEROR'S DECREE, THE PRINCE OF SPARTAX WILL BE HELD ACCOUNTABLE FOR ALL HIS CRIMES AGAINST THE EMPIRE. BOTH HIS AND THOSE OF HIS FELLOW TERRORIST PARTNERS.
WAIT.
KEEP MOVING, STAR-LORD.
HOLD-- JUST HOLD ON.
TELL MY FATHER--TELL HIM I CHANGED MY MIND.
WHAT SAY YOU?
MY FATHER SAID I EITHER STAND BY HIS SIDE AS THE PRINCE OF SPARTAX OR I SIT IN JAIL, OR WHATEVER YOU CALL JAIL, FOR THE REST OF MY LIFE.
I'M NOT COMPLETELY STUPID, I'LL DO IT.
I'LL BE THE FRICKIN' STAR-LORD.
THAT CHOICE HAS ALREADY BEEN MADE.
I'M SORRY... ARE YOU MY FATHER OR ARE YOU THE HELP?
TELL MY FATHER THAT I'M IN. I'LL BE STAR-LORD.
IF HE LETS THE REST OF THE GUARDIANS GO FREE. I'LL BE WHAT HE NEEDS ME TO BE.
IN RETURN, I PROMISE THE GUARDIANS WILL DISAPPEAR.
THEY WON'T GIVE SPARTAX ANY MORE TROUBLE. YOU HAVE MY WORD.
I BELIEVE WE ARE PAST THE POINT WHERE YOUR FATHER CAN MAKE THAT DEAL.
WHY?
WHERE ARE THE REST OF THE GUARDIANS?
I WILL CONVEY YOUR MESSAGE TO YOUR FATHER.
WHERE ARE THE GUARDIANS?!

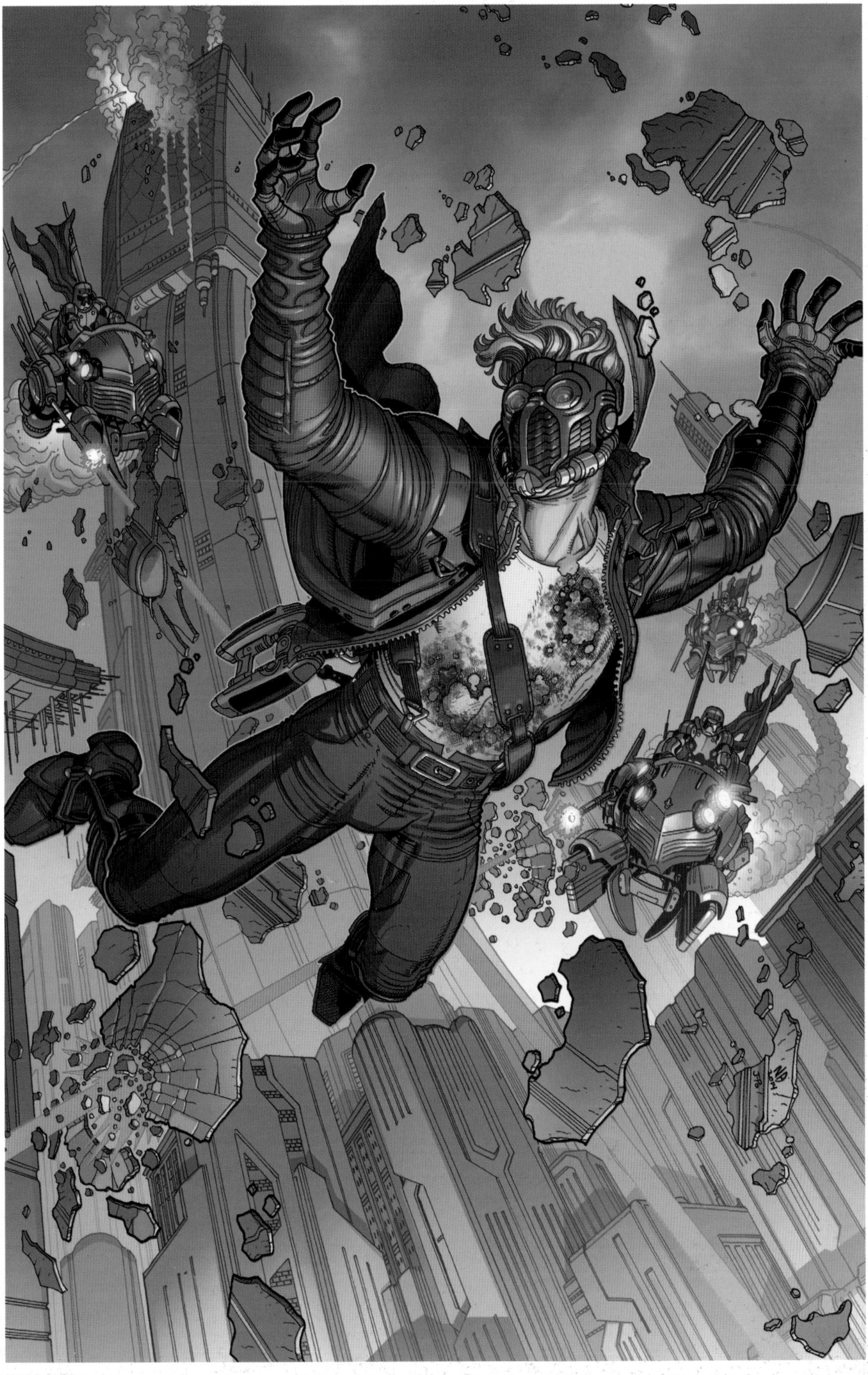

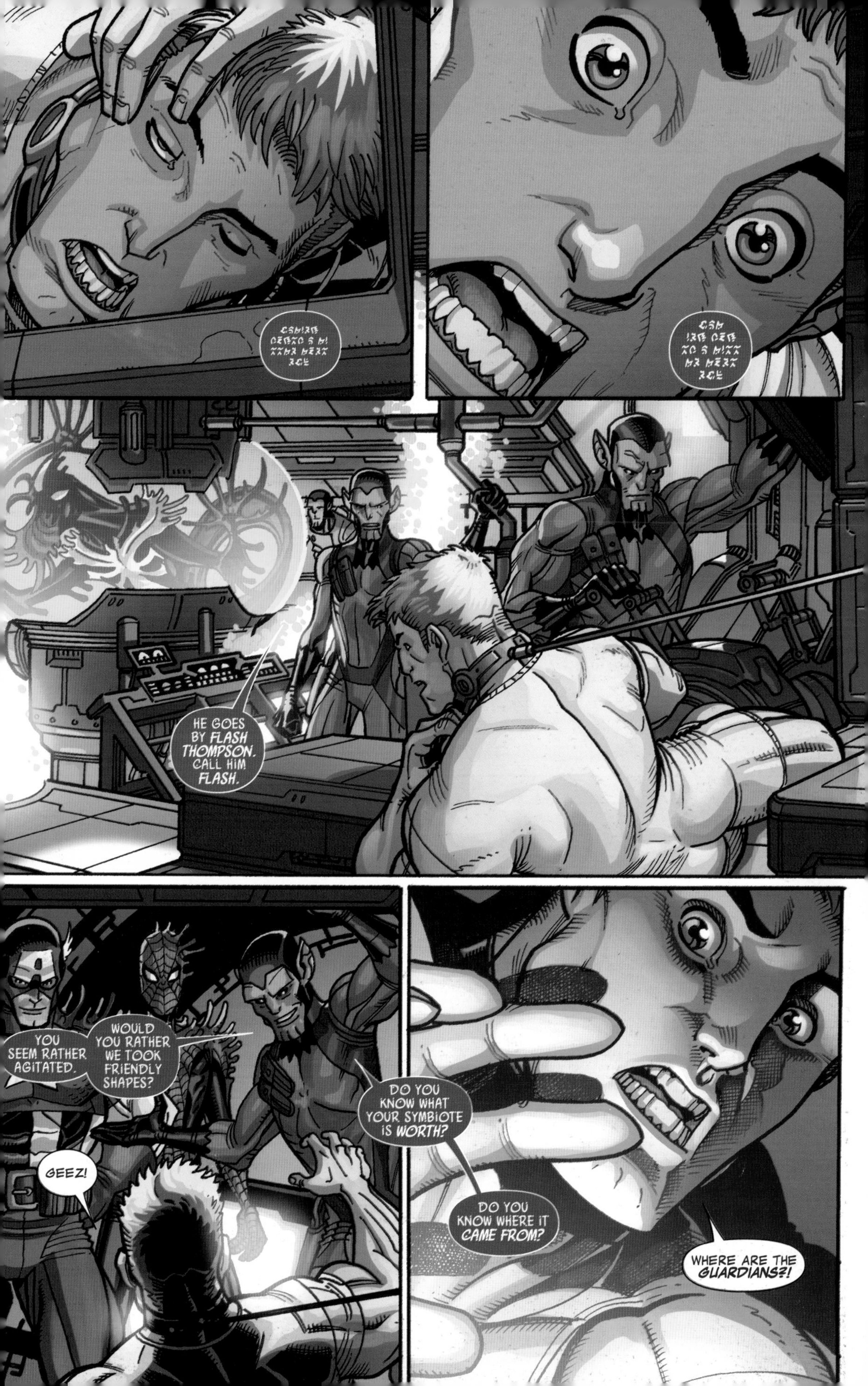
HE GOES BY FLASH THOMPSON. CALL HIM FLASH.
YOU SEEM RATHER AGITATED.
WOULD YOU RATHER WE TOOK FRIENDLY SHAPES?
GEEZ!
DO YOU KNOW WHAT YOUR SYMBIOTE IS WORTH?
DO YOU KNOW WHERE IT CAME FROM?
WHERE ARE THE GUARDIANS?!

THE IMPERIUM TRIBUNAL WILL NOW BE SILENT, FOR WE ARE ABOUT TO BEGIN!

THIS HUMAN WAS TRANSFORMED INTO THIS--THIS SO-CALLED "DESTROYER"--FOR THE SOLE PURPOSE OF ATTACKING AND KILLING THE MAD TITAN *THANOS*.

BUT INSTEAD HE HAS CHOSEN TO USE HIS GIFTS FOR TERRORISM AND THIEVERY.

ALL THIS IS *FACT*.

BUT HE IS HERE TO ANSWER FOR HIS PART IN OBSTRUCTING OUR WAY OF JUSTICE AND HIS ALLIANCE WITH THE EARTH PHOENIX VESSEL KNOWN AS *JEAN GREY*.

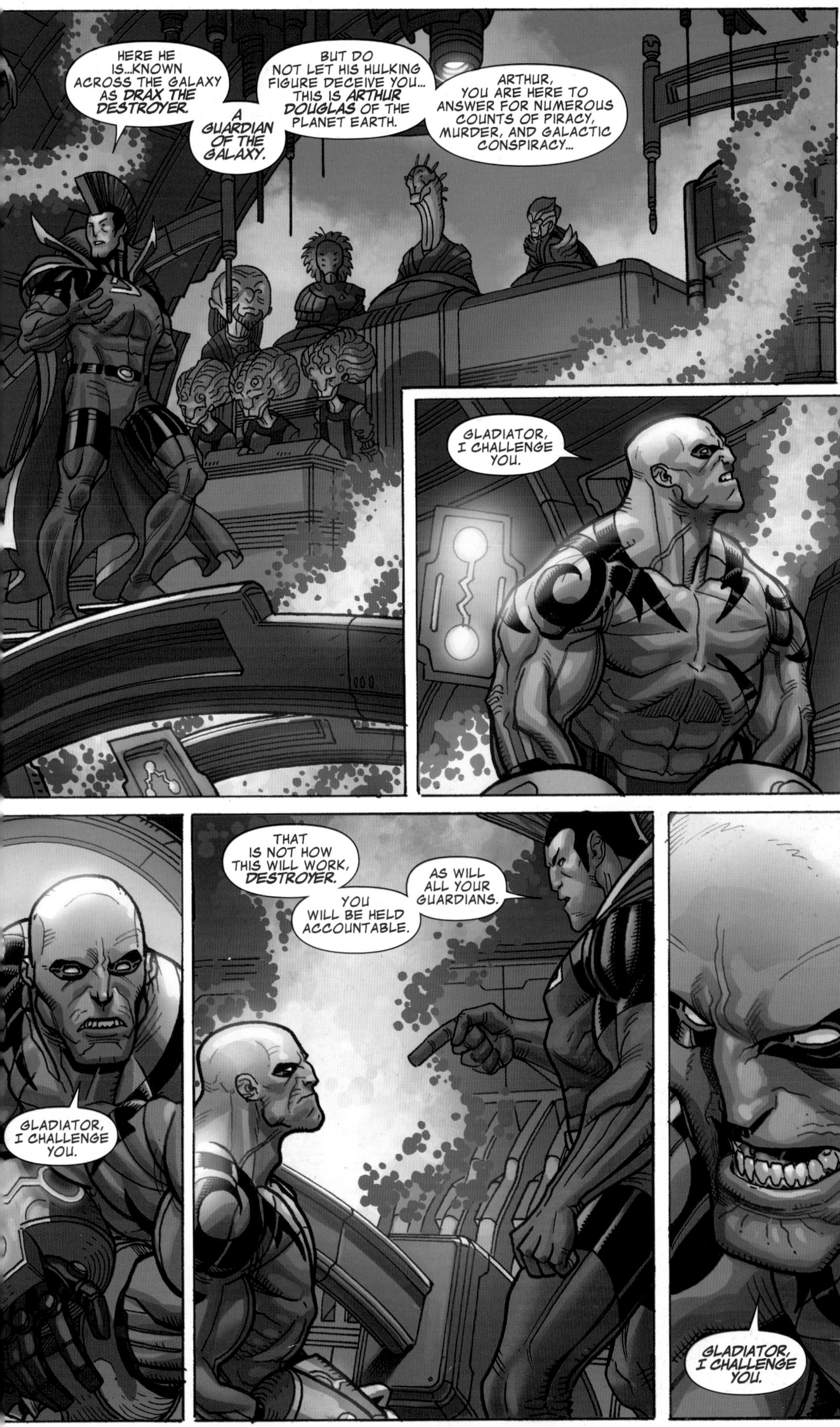
HERE HE IS...KNOWN ACROSS THE GALAXY AS DRAX THE DESTROYER.
A GUARDIAN OF THE GALAXY.
BUT DO NOT LET HIS HULKING FIGURE DECEIVE YOU... THIS IS ARTHUR DOUGLAS OF THE PLANET EARTH.
ARTHUR, YOU ARE HERE TO ANSWER FOR NUMEROUS COUNTS OF PIRACY, MURDER, AND GALACTIC CONSPIRACY...
GLADIATOR, I CHALLENGE YOU.
GLADIATOR, I CHALLENGE YOU.
THAT IS NOT HOW THIS WILL WORK, DESTROYER.
YOU WILL BE HELD ACCOUNTABLE.
AS WILL ALL YOUR GUARDIANS.
GLADIATOR, I CHALLENGE YOU.

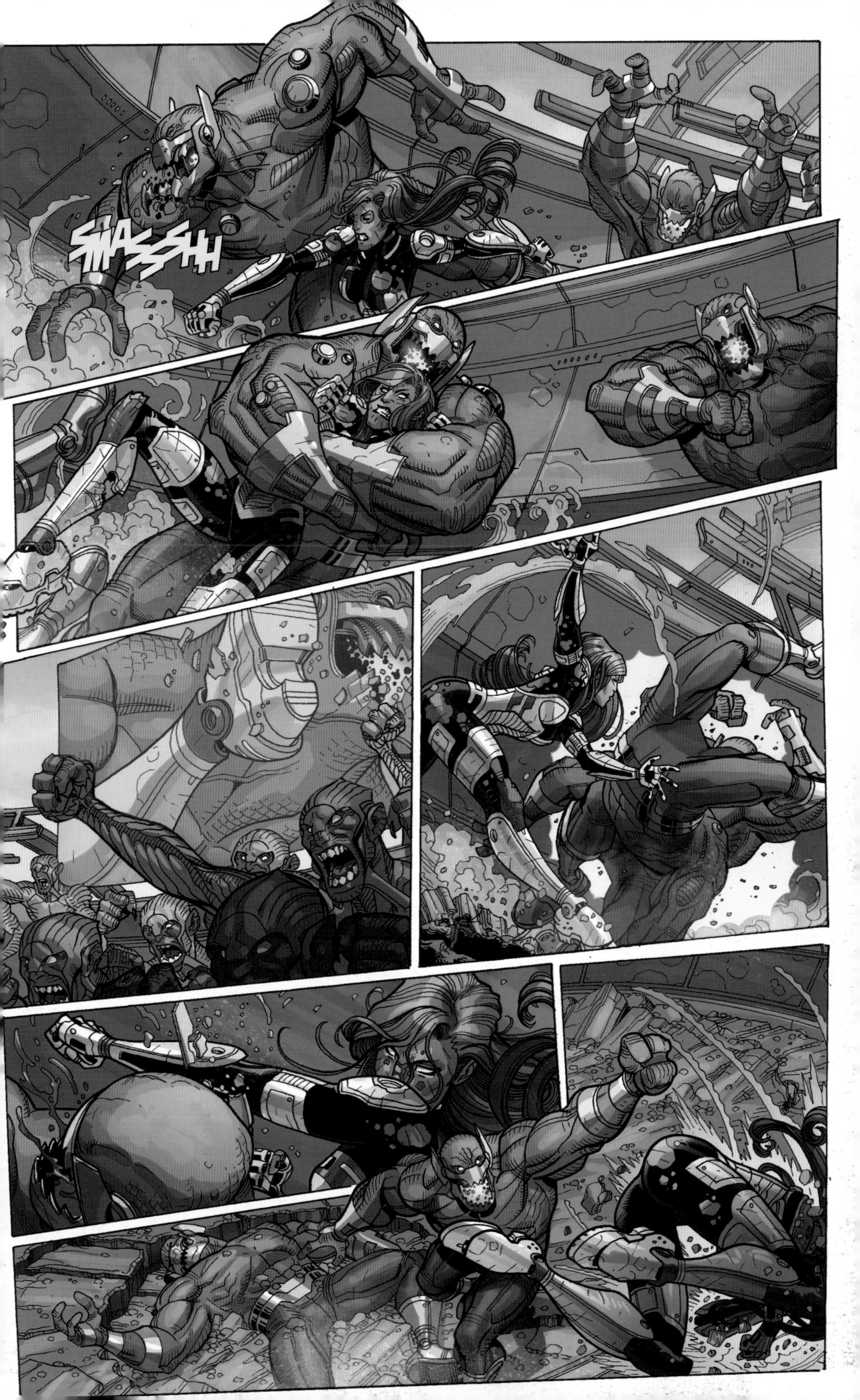
SMASSHH

I FIND MYSELF SURPRISED TO SAY THIS, BUT I TIRE OF HER TORTURE.

FINISH HER.

IF THIS BE MY TIME, THEN SO BE IT.

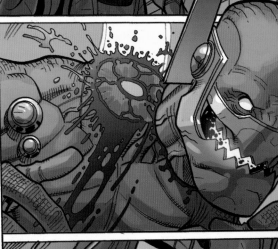

YOU.

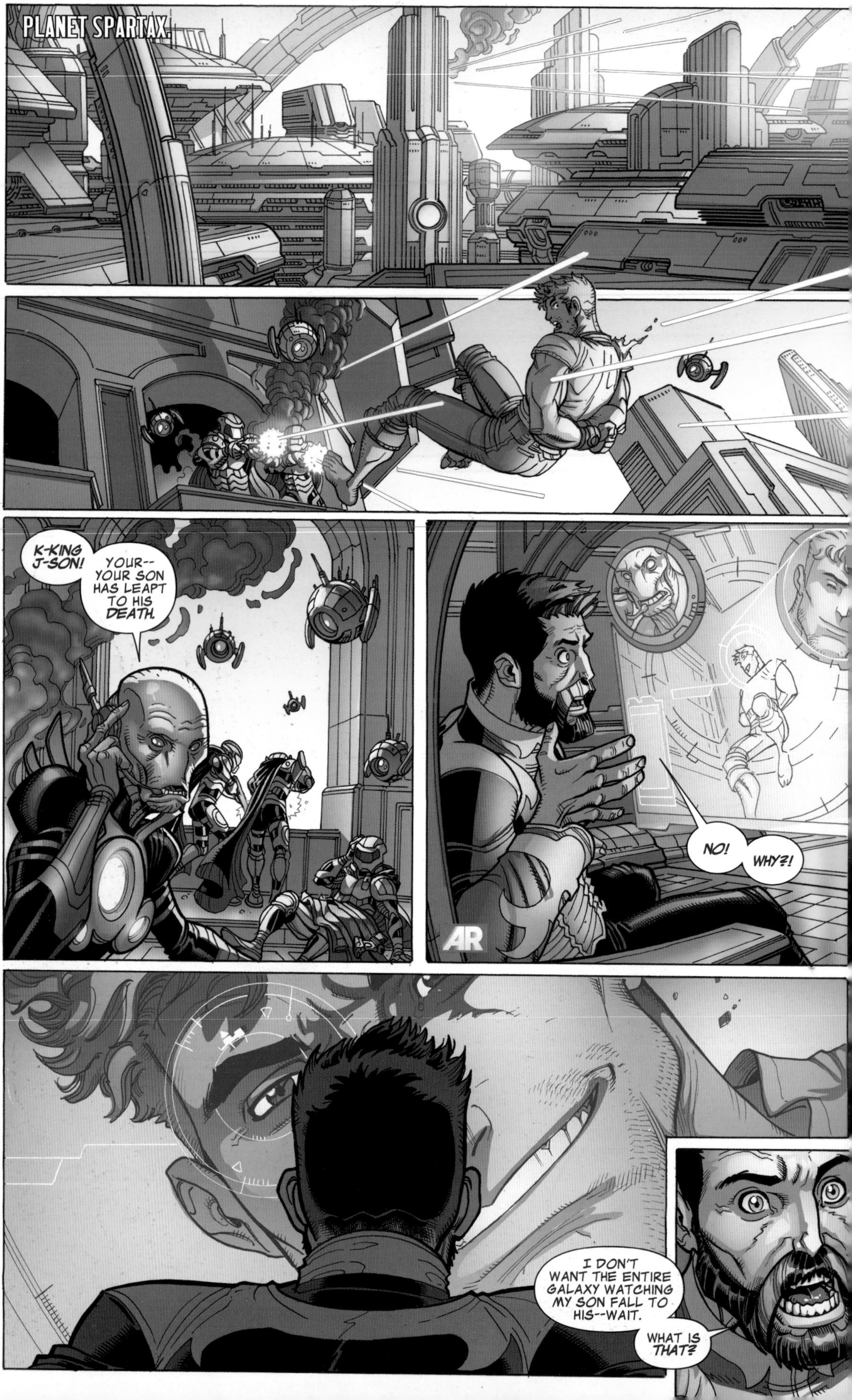
PLANET SPARTAX.
K-KING J-SON!
YOUR-- YOUR SON HAS LEAPT TO HIS DEATH.
NO!
WHY?!
I DON'T WANT THE ENTIRE GALAXY WATCHING MY SON FALL TO HIS--WAIT.
WHAT IS THAT?

ZZZWAATTECCKKTTT

THE GUN IS SET TO ME AND ME ONLY, GENIUS.

I'M THE FRICKIN' STAR-LORD AND YOU'RE A SPARTAX ROYAL GUARD.

YOU SHOULD HAVE KNOWN THAT.

FSSHHAAMM

LET'S GET YOUR STUFF AND GET OUT OF HERE!

GO FIND THE OTHER GUARDIANS.

NUH-UH. NOT YET.

HI.

WHERE ARE THE OTHER GUARDIANS OF THE GALAXY?

AND MY PANTS?

YOU--YOU'LL HAVE TO A-ASK YOUR FATHER.

I'M ASKING YOU.

WHAT DID YOU DO TO THE GUARDIANS?

STAND DOWN, STAR-LORD!

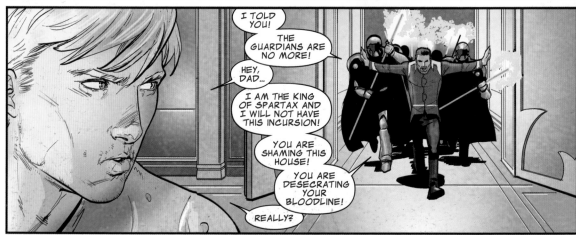

I TOLD YOU!

THE GUARDIANS ARE NO MORE!

HEY, DAD...

I AM THE KING OF SPARTAX AND I WILL NOT HAVE THIS INCURSION!

YOU ARE SHAMING THIS HOUSE!

YOU ARE DESECRATING YOUR BLOODLINE!

REALLY?

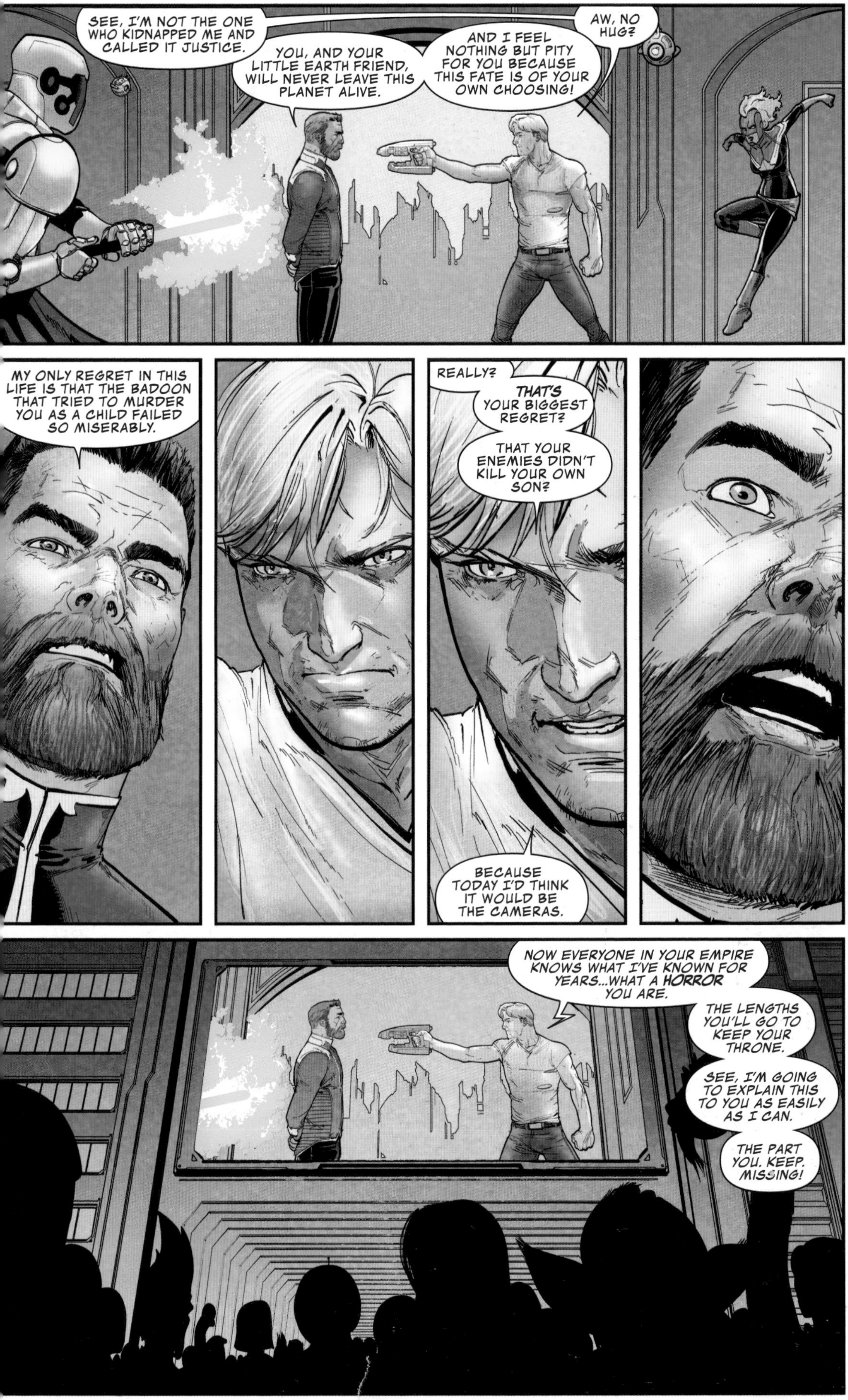
SEE, I'M NOT THE ONE WHO KIDNAPPED ME AND CALLED IT JUSTICE.
AW, NO HUG?
YOU, AND YOUR LITTLE EARTH FRIEND, WILL NEVER LEAVE THIS PLANET ALIVE.
AND I FEEL NOTHING BUT PITY FOR YOU BECAUSE THIS FATE IS OF YOUR OWN CHOOSING!
MY ONLY REGRET IN THIS LIFE IS THAT THE BADOON THAT TRIED TO MURDER YOU AS A CHILD FAILED SO MISERABLY.
REALLY?
THAT'S YOUR BIGGEST REGRET?
THAT YOUR ENEMIES DIDN'T KILL YOUR OWN SON?
BECAUSE TODAY I'D THINK IT WOULD BE THE CAMERAS.
NOW EVERYONE IN YOUR EMPIRE KNOWS WHAT I'VE KNOWN FOR YEARS...WHAT A HORROR YOU ARE.
THE LENGTHS YOU'LL GO TO KEEP YOUR THRONE.
SEE, I'M GOING TO EXPLAIN THIS TO YOU AS EASILY AS I CAN.
THE PART YOU. KEEP. MISSING!

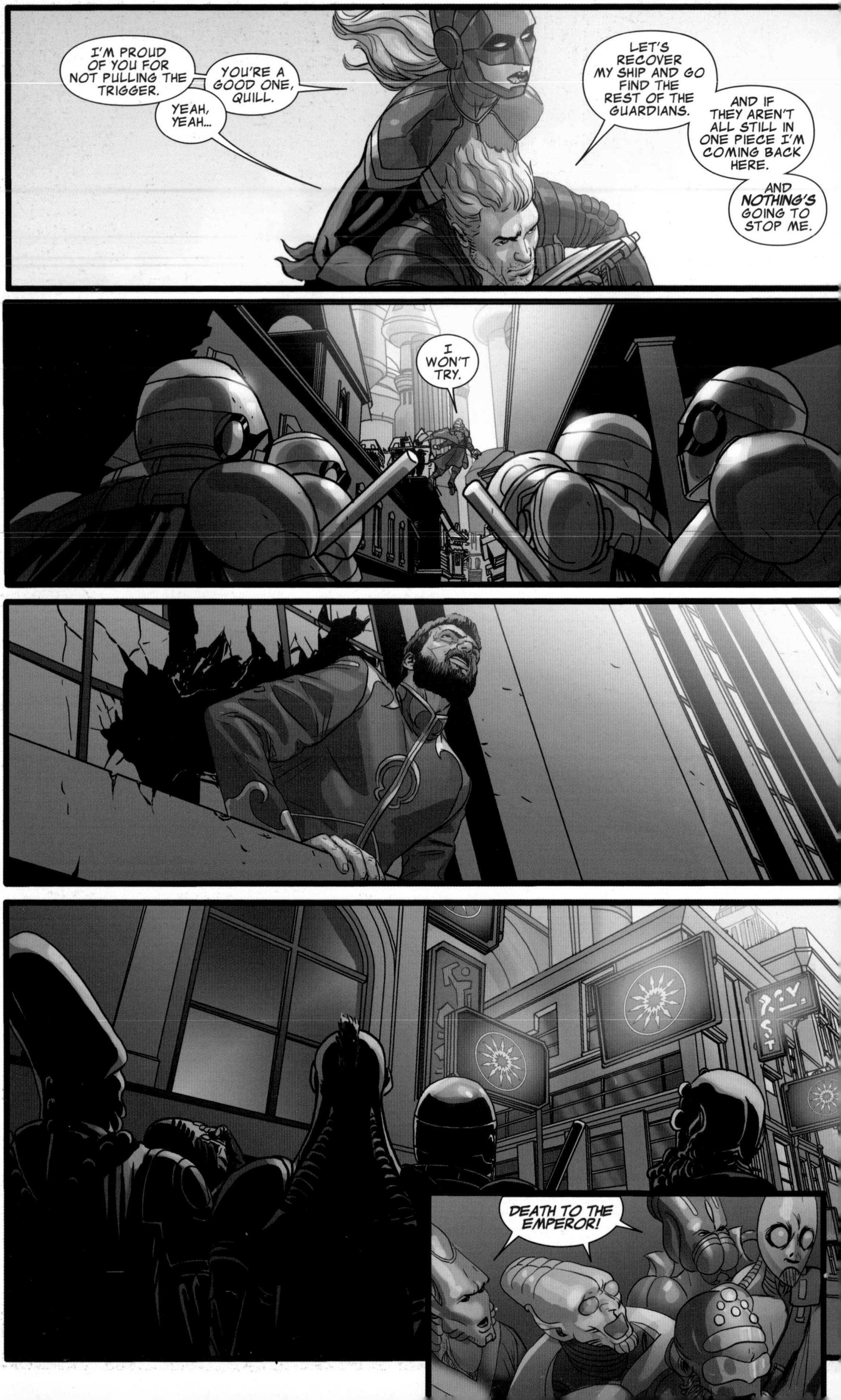
I'M PROUD OF YOU FOR NOT PULLING THE TRIGGER.
YOU'RE A GOOD ONE, QUILL.
YEAH, YEAH...
LET'S RECOVER MY SHIP AND GO FIND THE REST OF THE GUARDIANS.
AND IF THEY AREN'T ALL STILL IN ONE PIECE I'M COMING BACK HERE.
AND NOTHING'S GOING TO STOP ME.
I WON'T TRY.
DEATH TO THE EMPEROR!

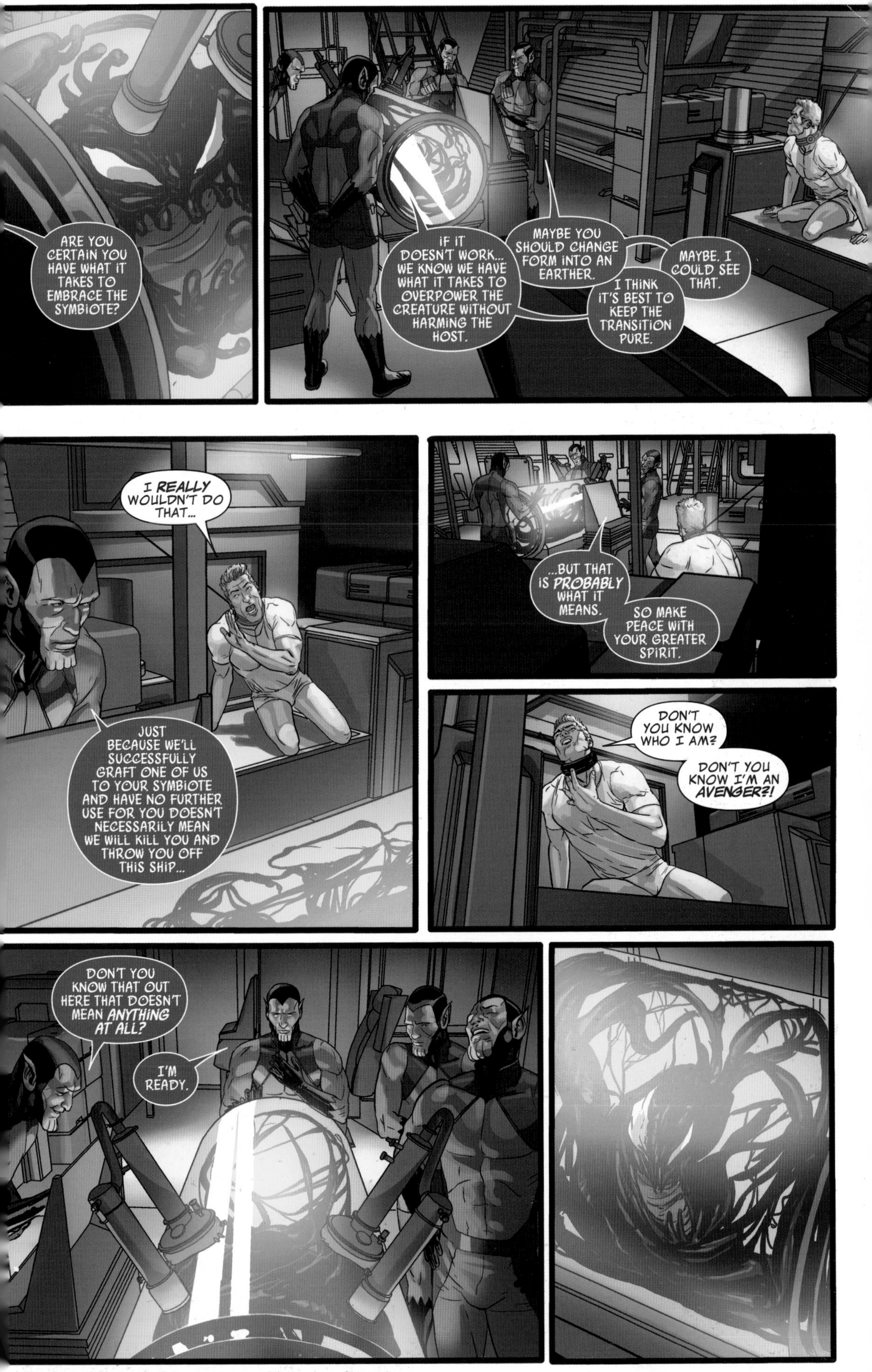
ARE YOU CERTAIN YOU HAVE WHAT IT TAKES TO EMBRACE THE SYMBIOTE?
IF IT DOESN'T WORK... WE KNOW WE HAVE WHAT IT TAKES TO OVERPOWER THE CREATURE WITHOUT HARMING THE HOST.
MAYBE YOU SHOULD CHANGE FORM INTO AN EARTHER.
I THINK IT'S BEST TO KEEP THE TRANSITION PURE.
MAYBE. I COULD SEE THAT.
I REALLY WOULDN'T DO THAT...
JUST BECAUSE WE'LL SUCCESSFULLY GRAFT ONE OF US TO YOUR SYMBIOTE AND HAVE NO FURTHER USE FOR YOU DOESN'T NECESSARILY MEAN WE WILL KILL YOU AND THROW YOU OFF THIS SHIP...
...BUT THAT IS PROBABLY WHAT IT MEANS.
SO MAKE PEACE WITH YOUR GREATER SPIRIT.
DON'T YOU KNOW WHO I AM?
DON'T YOU KNOW I'M AN AVENGER?!
DON'T YOU KNOW THAT OUT HERE THAT DOESN'T MEAN ANYTHING AT ALL?
I'M READY.

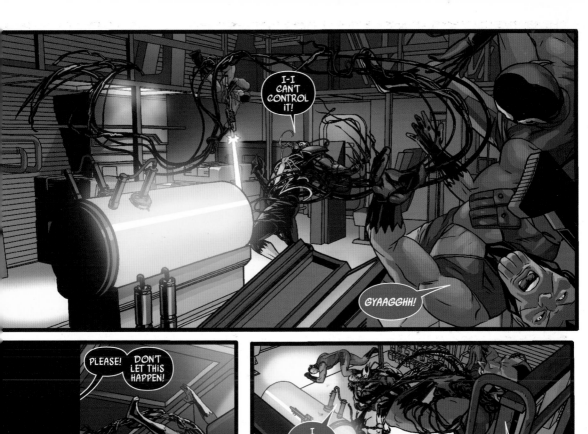

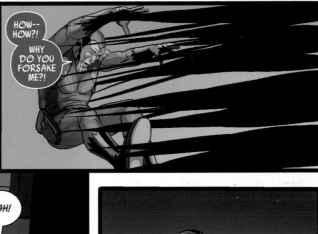

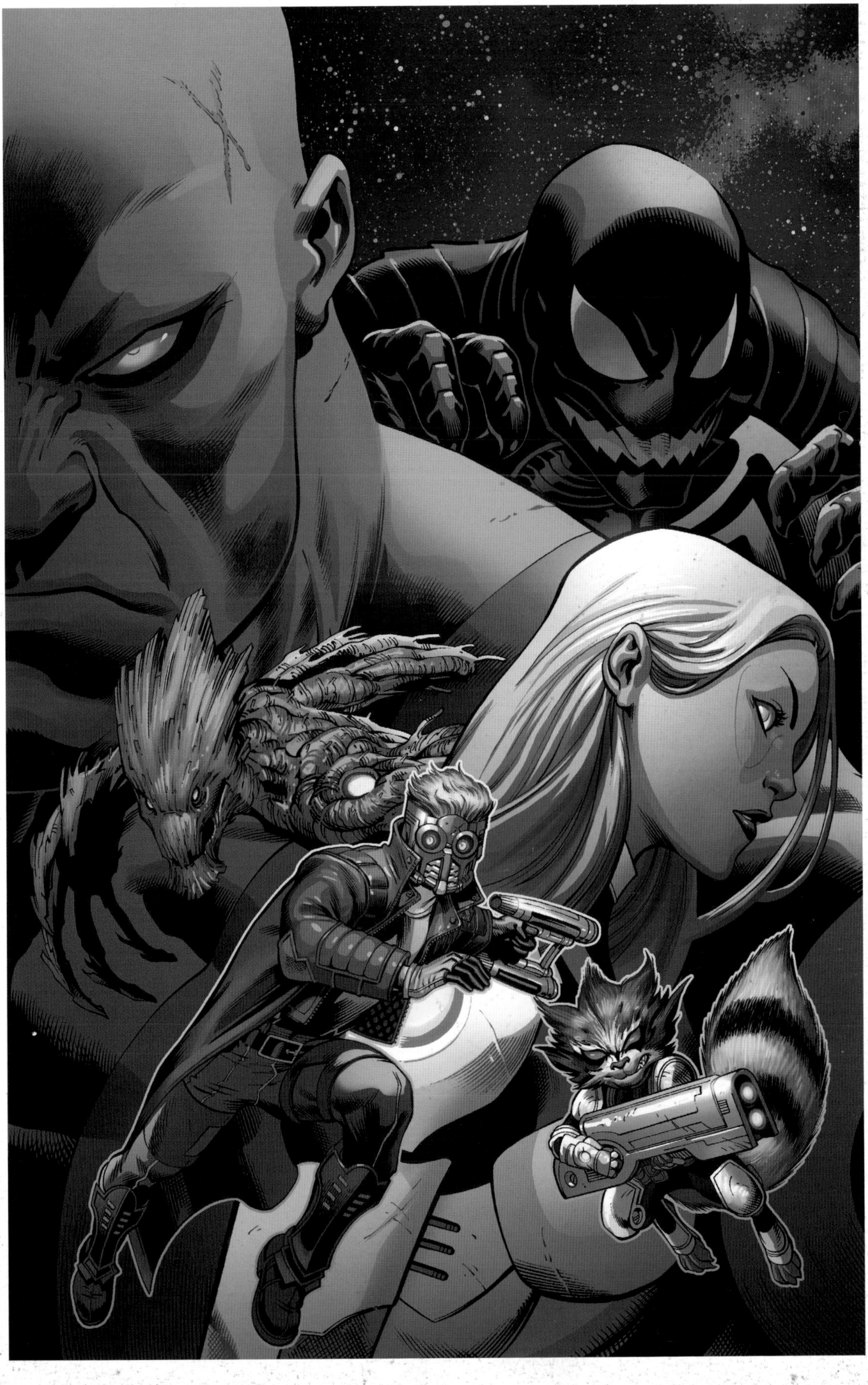

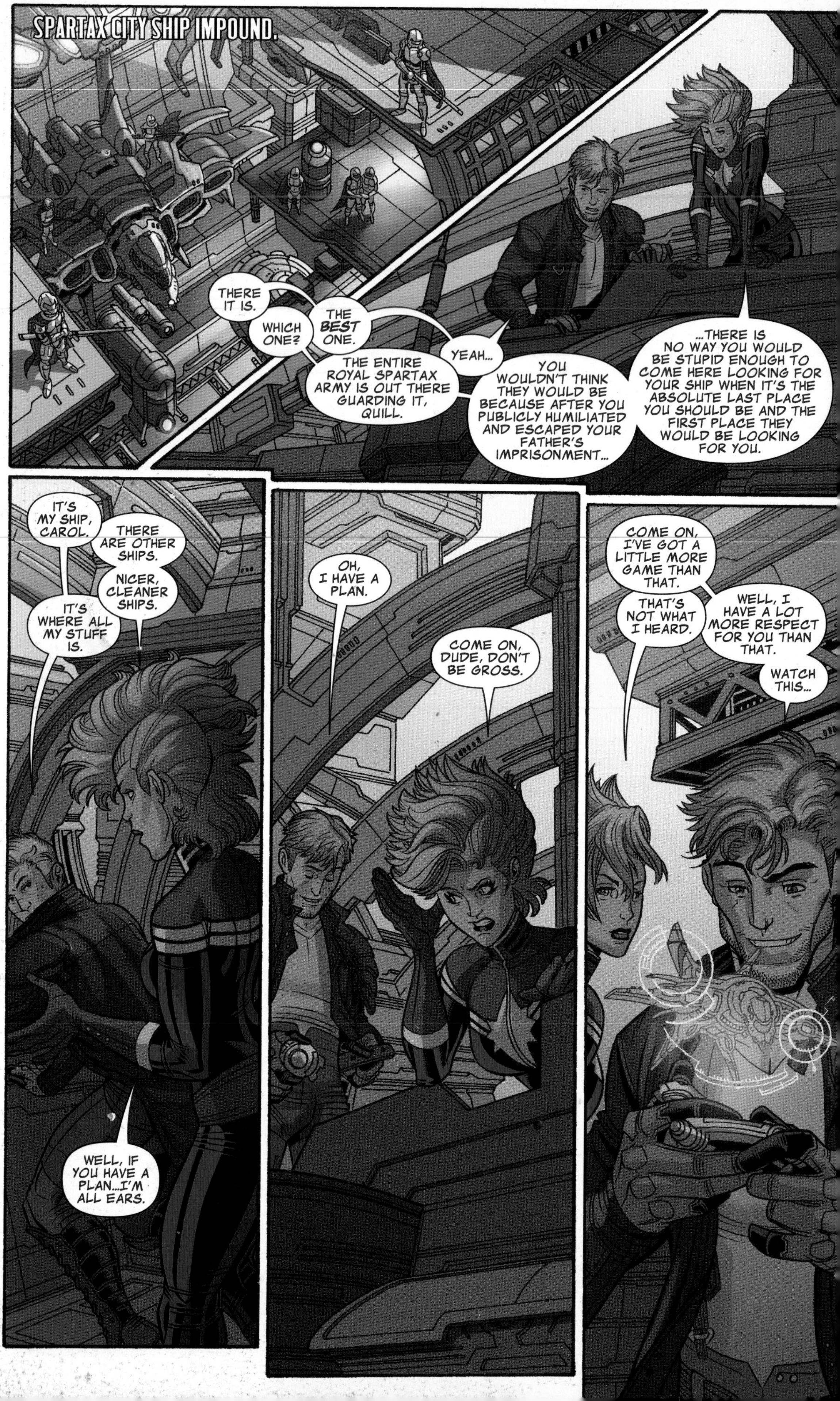
SPARTAX CITY SHIP IMPOUND.
THERE IT IS.
WHICH ONE?
THE BEST ONE.
YEAH...
THE ENTIRE ROYAL SPARTAX ARMY IS OUT THERE GUARDING IT, QUILL.
YOU WOULDN'T THINK THEY WOULD BE BECAUSE AFTER YOU PUBLICLY HUMILIATED AND ESCAPED YOUR FATHER'S IMPRISONMENT...
...THERE IS NO WAY YOU WOULD BE STUPID ENOUGH TO COME HERE LOOKING FOR YOUR SHIP WHEN IT'S THE ABSOLUTE LAST PLACE YOU SHOULD BE AND THE FIRST PLACE THEY WOULD BE LOOKING FOR YOU.
IT'S MY SHIP, CAROL.
THERE ARE OTHER SHIPS.
NICER, CLEANER SHIPS.
IT'S WHERE ALL MY STUFF IS.
WELL, IF YOU HAVE A PLAN...I'M ALL EARS.
OH, I HAVE A PLAN.
COME ON, DUDE, DON'T BE GROSS.
COME ON, I'VE GOT A LITTLE MORE GAME THAN THAT.
THAT'S NOT WHAT I HEARD.
WELL, I HAVE A LOT MORE RESPECT FOR YOU THAN THAT.
WATCH THIS...

ROYAL AIR GUARD! PULL BACK!

TELL THE ROYAL SHIPS TO PULL BACK!

CR-UHH TNWH

YOUR HIGHNESS, WE HAVE TO GET YOU OUT OF HERE!

MY SON IS NOT COMING BACK.

HE MADE HIS POINT.

IT'S NOT YOUR SON, SIR...

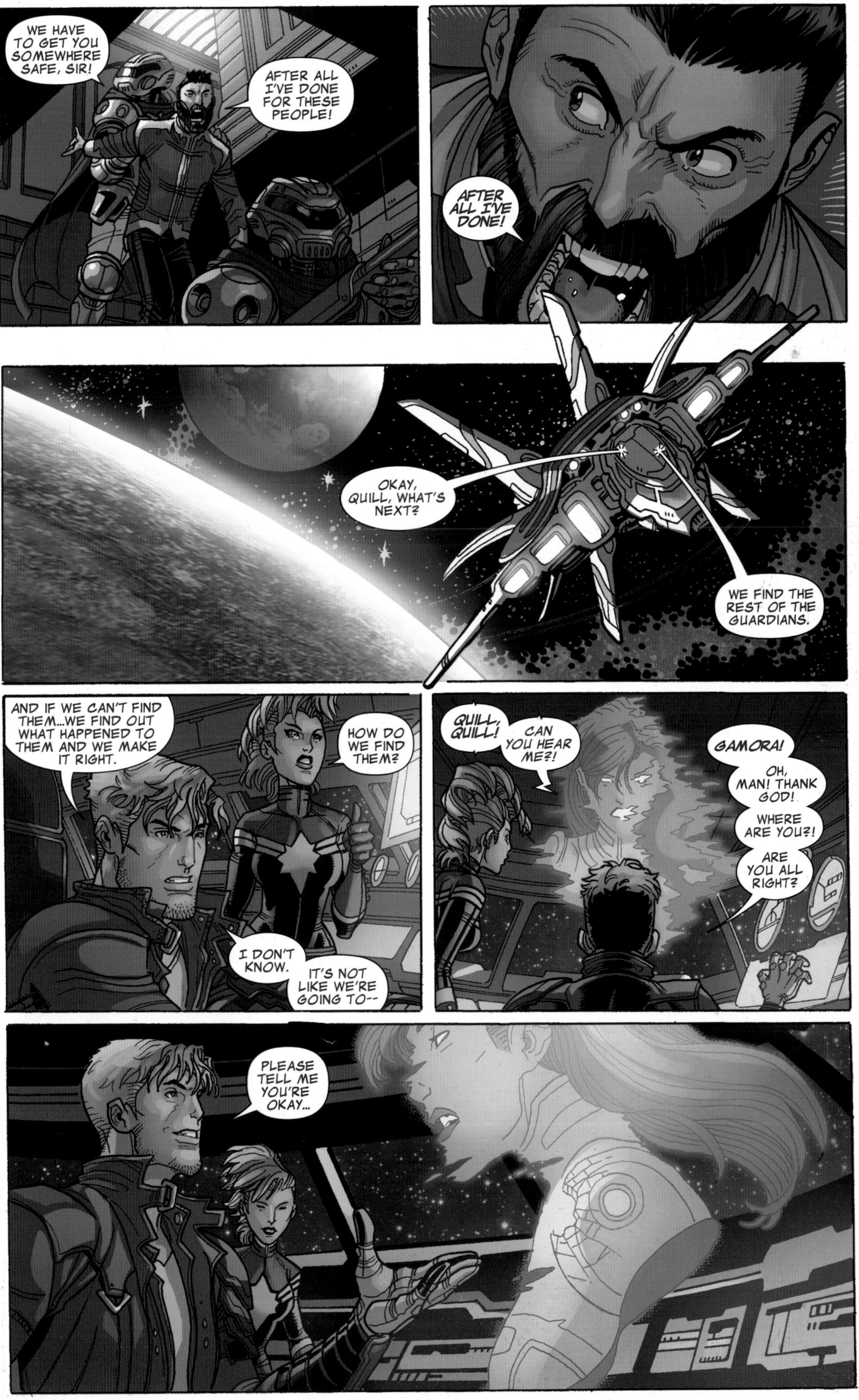
WE HAVE TO GET YOU SOMEWHERE SAFE, SIR!
AFTER ALL I'VE DONE FOR THESE PEOPLE!
AFTER ALL I'VE DONE!
OKAY, QUILL, WHAT'S NEXT?
WE FIND THE REST OF THE GUARDIANS.
AND IF WE CAN'T FIND THEM...WE FIND OUT WHAT HAPPENED TO THEM AND WE MAKE IT RIGHT.
HOW DO WE FIND THEM?
I DON'T KNOW.
IT'S NOT LIKE WE'RE GOING TO--
QUILL, QUILL!
CAN YOU HEAR ME?!
GAMORA!
OH, MAN! THANK GOD!
WHERE ARE YOU?!
ARE YOU ALL RIGHT?
PLEASE TELL ME YOU'RE OKAY...

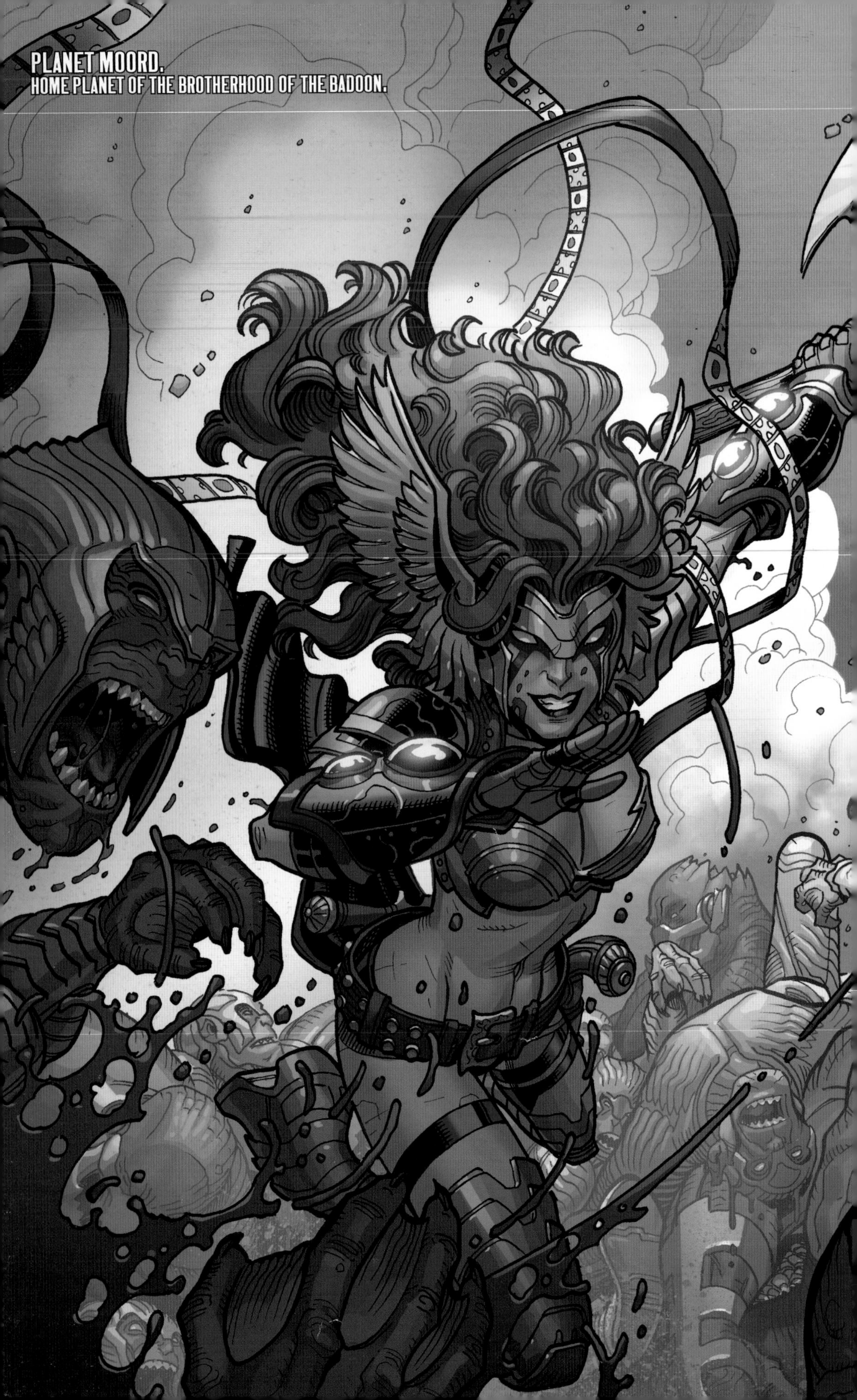
PLANET MOORD.
HOME PLANET OF THE BROTHERHOOD OF THE BADOON.

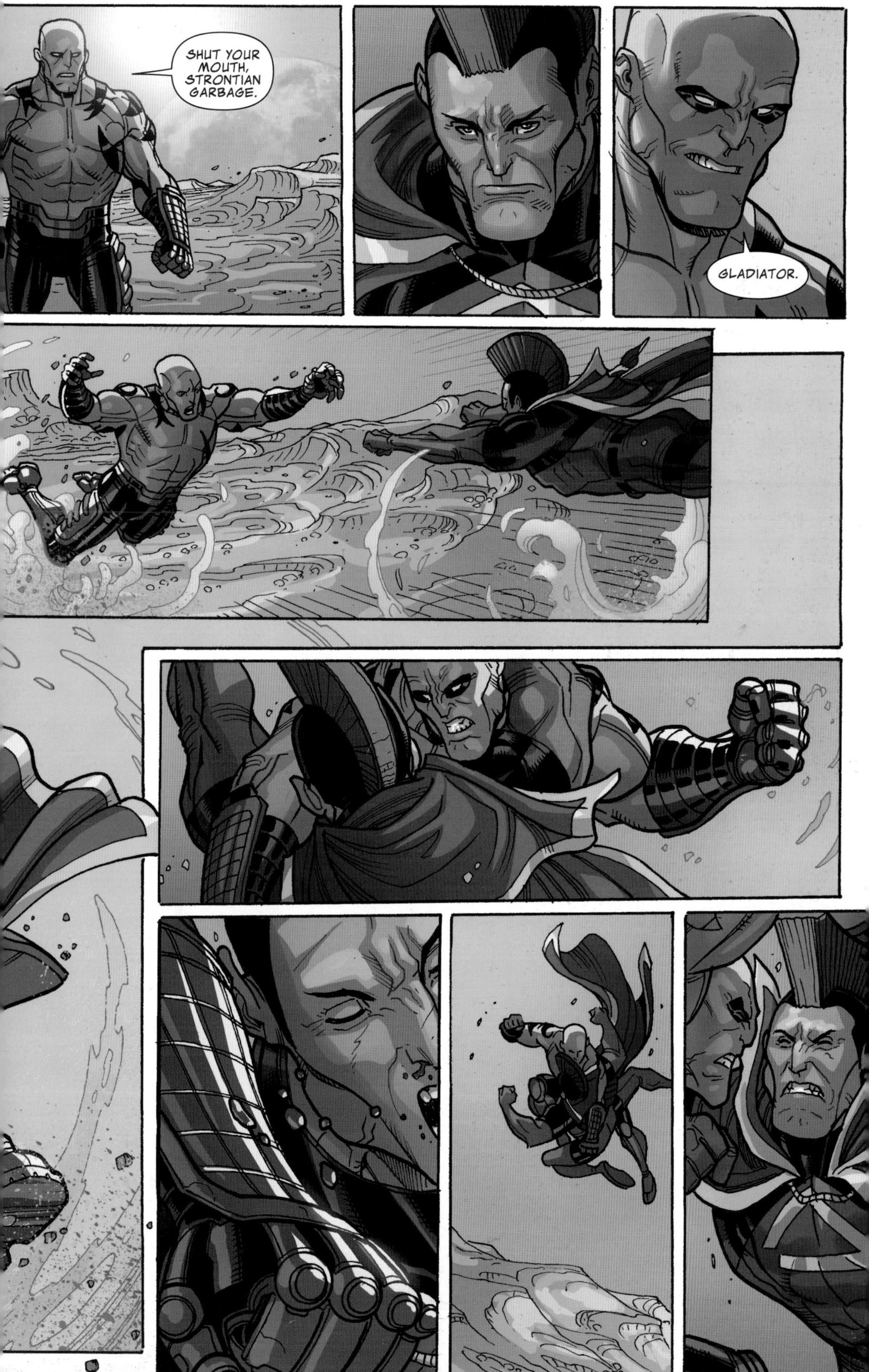
SHUT YOUR MOUTH, STRONTIAN GARBAGE.
GLADIATOR.

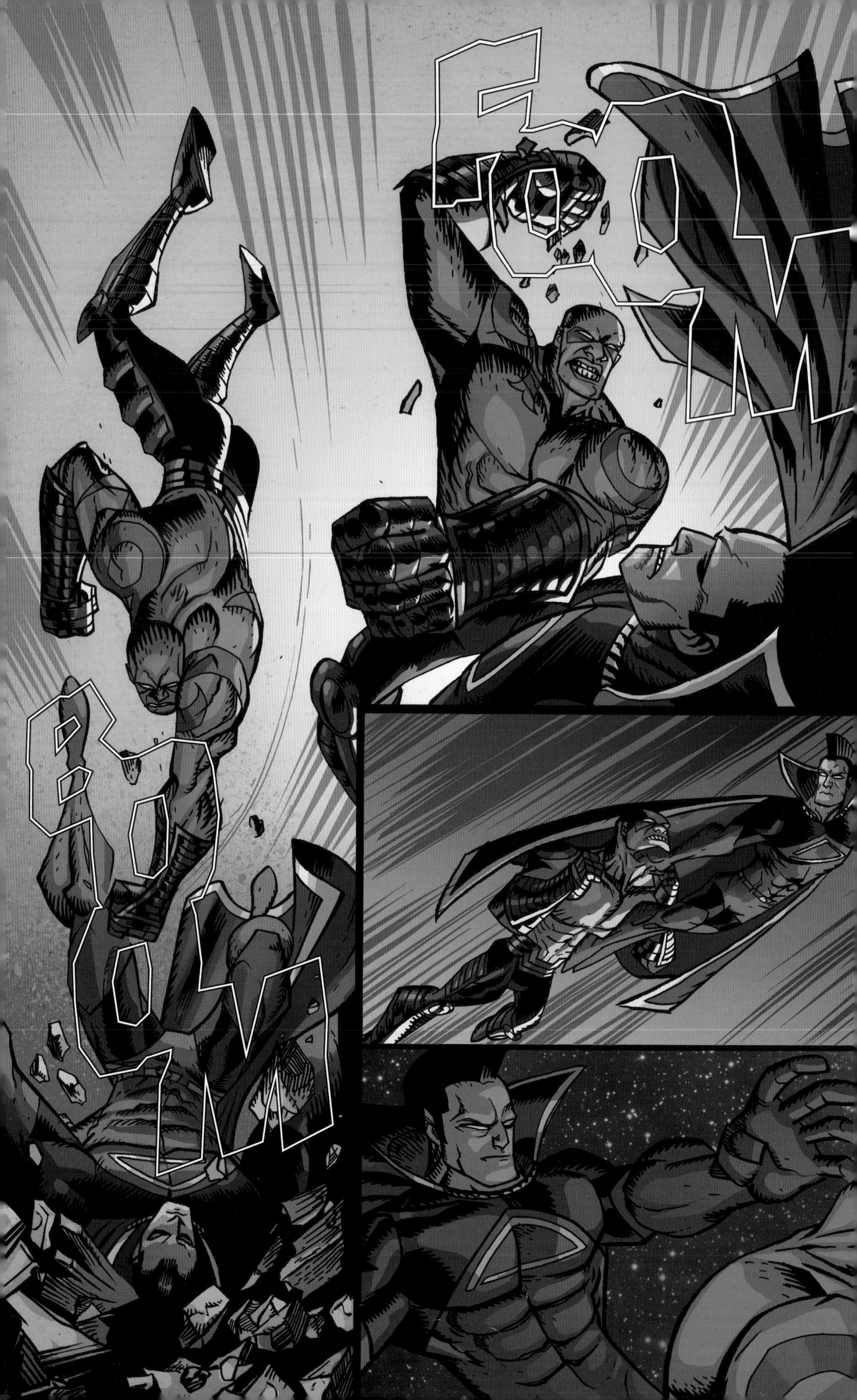
FOOOM
BOOOM

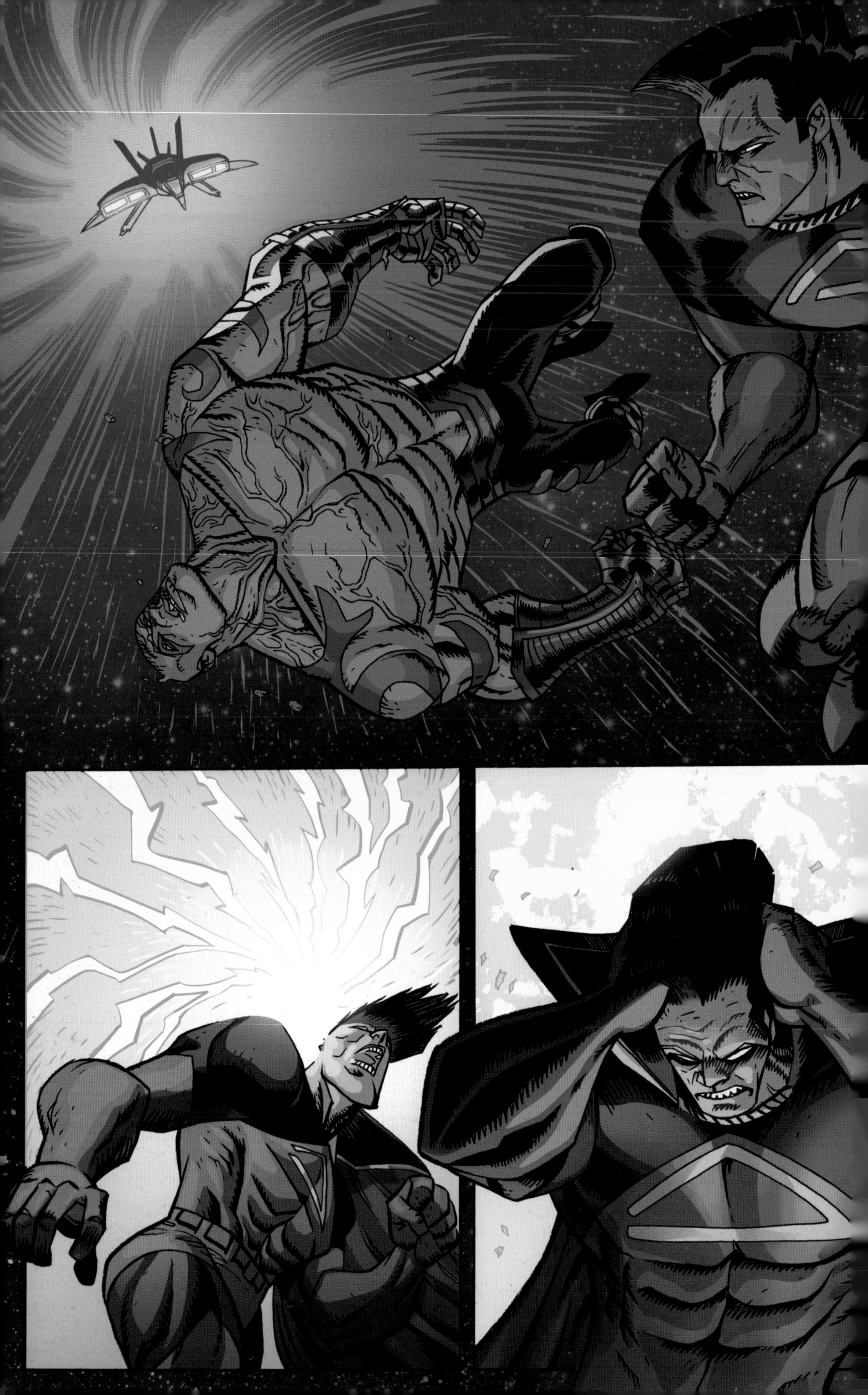

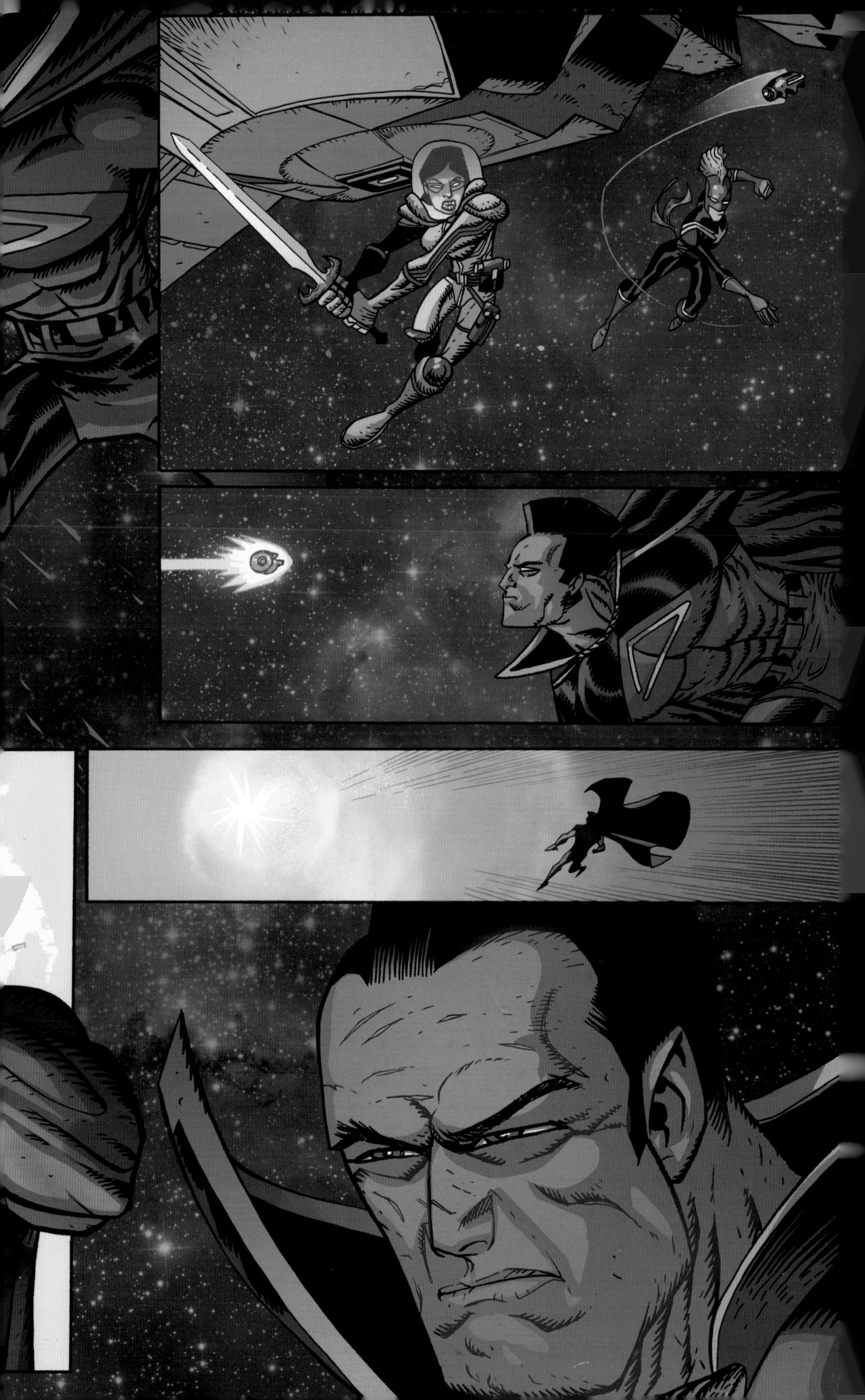

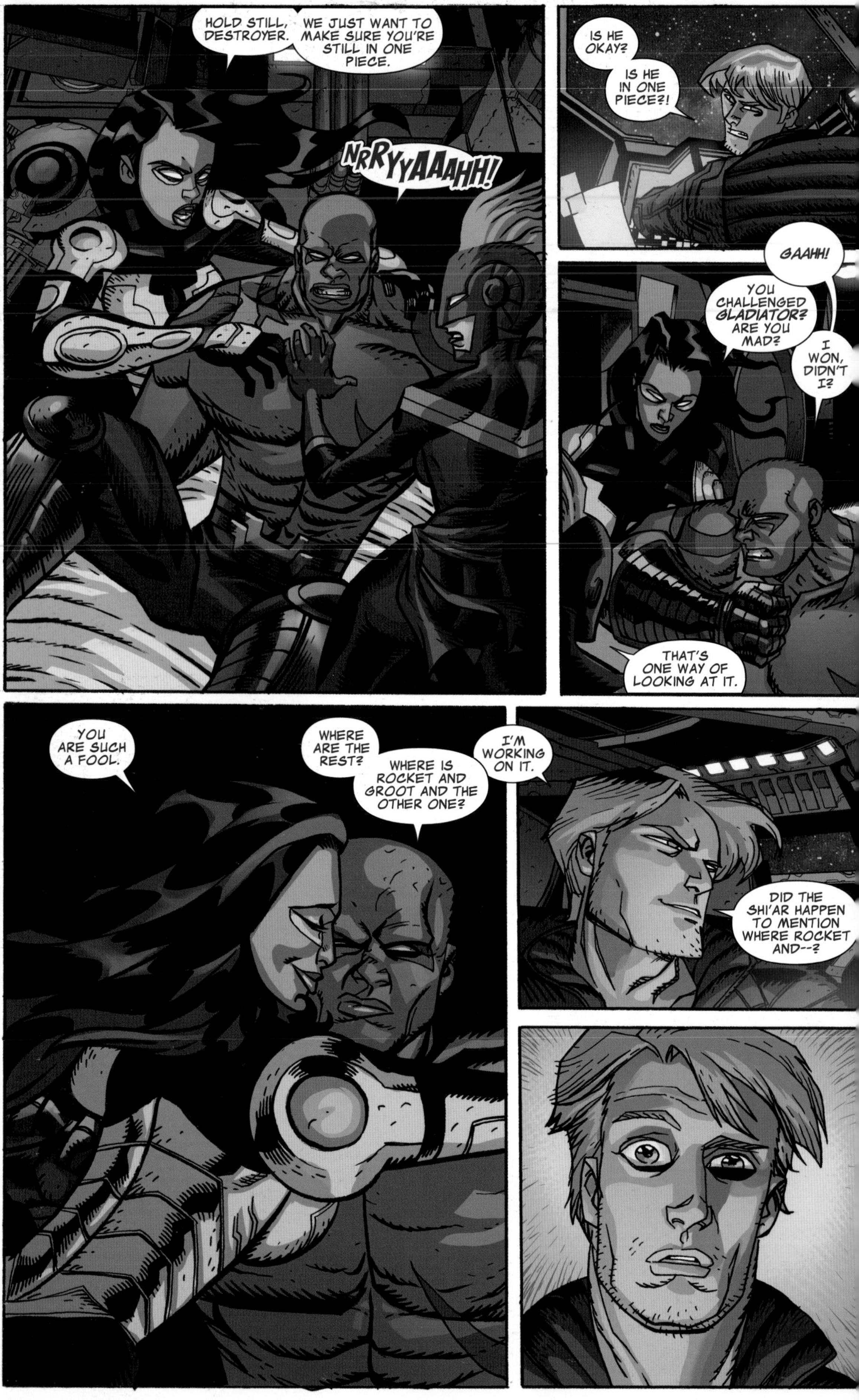
HOLD STILL, DESTROYER.
WE JUST WANT TO MAKE SURE YOU'RE STILL IN ONE PIECE.
NRRYYAAAHH!
IS HE OKAY?
IS HE IN ONE PIECE?!
GAAHH!
YOU CHALLENGED GLADIATOR? ARE YOU MAD?
I WON, DIDN'T I?
THAT'S ONE WAY OF LOOKING AT IT.
YOU ARE SUCH A FOOL.
WHERE ARE THE REST?
WHERE IS ROCKET AND GROOT AND THE OTHER ONE?
I'M WORKING ON IT.
DID THE SHI'AR HAPPEN TO MENTION WHERE ROCKET AND--?

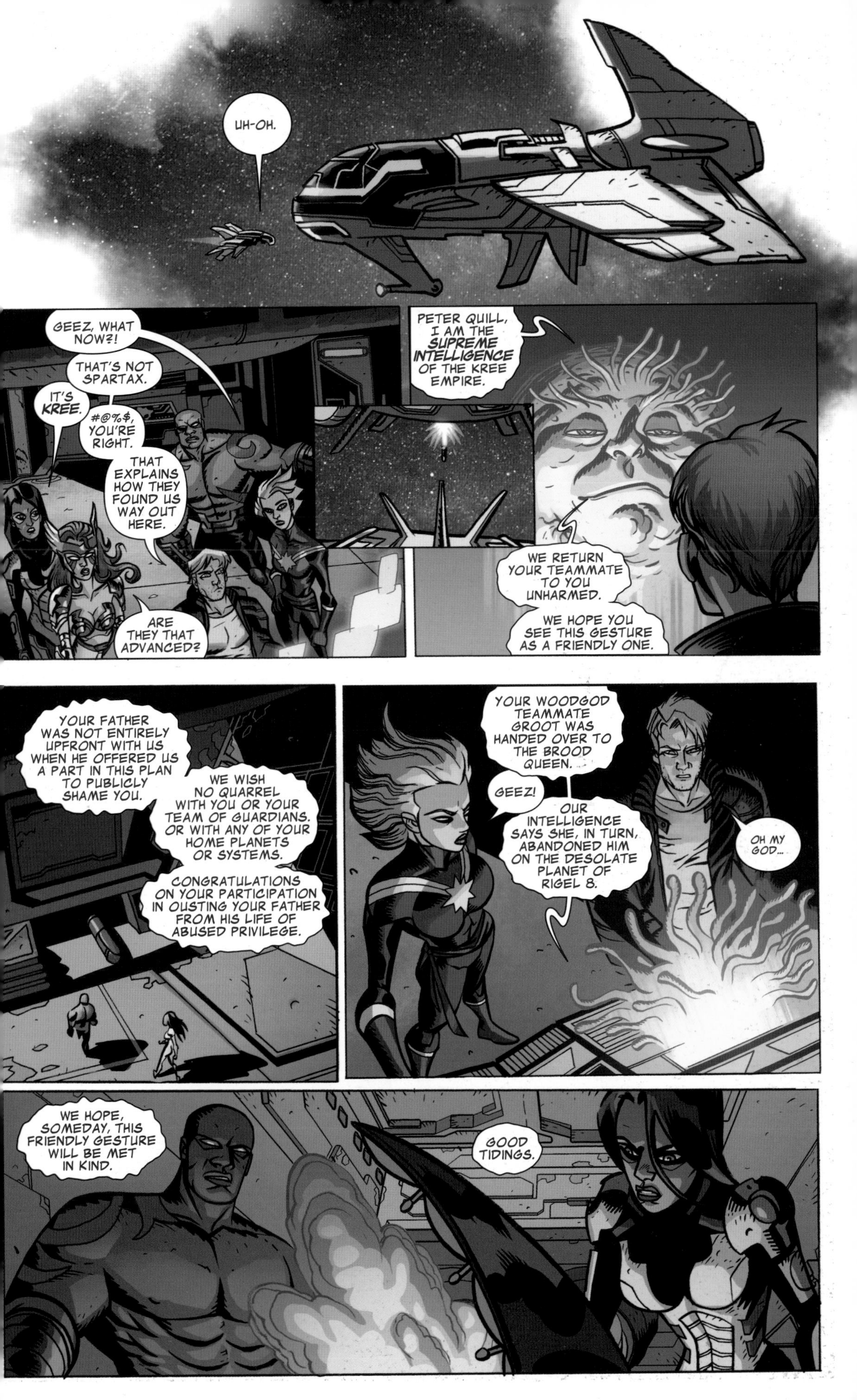
UH-OH.
GEEZ, WHAT NOW?!
THAT'S NOT SPARTAX.
IT'S KREE.
#@%$, YOU'RE RIGHT.
THAT EXPLAINS HOW THEY FOUND US WAY OUT HERE.
ARE THEY THAT ADVANCED?
PETER QUILL, I AM THE SUPREME INTELLIGENCE OF THE KREE EMPIRE.
WE RETURN YOUR TEAMMATE TO YOU UNHARMED.
WE HOPE YOU SEE THIS GESTURE AS A FRIENDLY ONE.
YOUR FATHER WAS NOT ENTIRELY UPFRONT WITH US WHEN HE OFFERED US A PART IN THIS PLAN TO PUBLICLY SHAME YOU.
WE WISH NO QUARREL WITH YOU OR YOUR TEAM OF GUARDIANS. OR WITH ANY OF YOUR HOME PLANETS OR SYSTEMS.
CONGRATULATIONS ON YOUR PARTICIPATION IN OUSTING YOUR FATHER FROM HIS LIFE OF ABUSED PRIVILEGE.
YOUR WOODGOD TEAMMATE GROOT WAS HANDED OVER TO THE BROOD QUEEN.
GEEZ!
OUR INTELLIGENCE SAYS SHE, IN TURN, ABANDONED HIM ON THE DESOLATE PLANET OF RIGEL 8.
OH MY GOD...
WE HOPE, SOMEDAY, THIS FRIENDLY GESTURE WILL BE MET IN KIND.
GOOD TIDINGS.

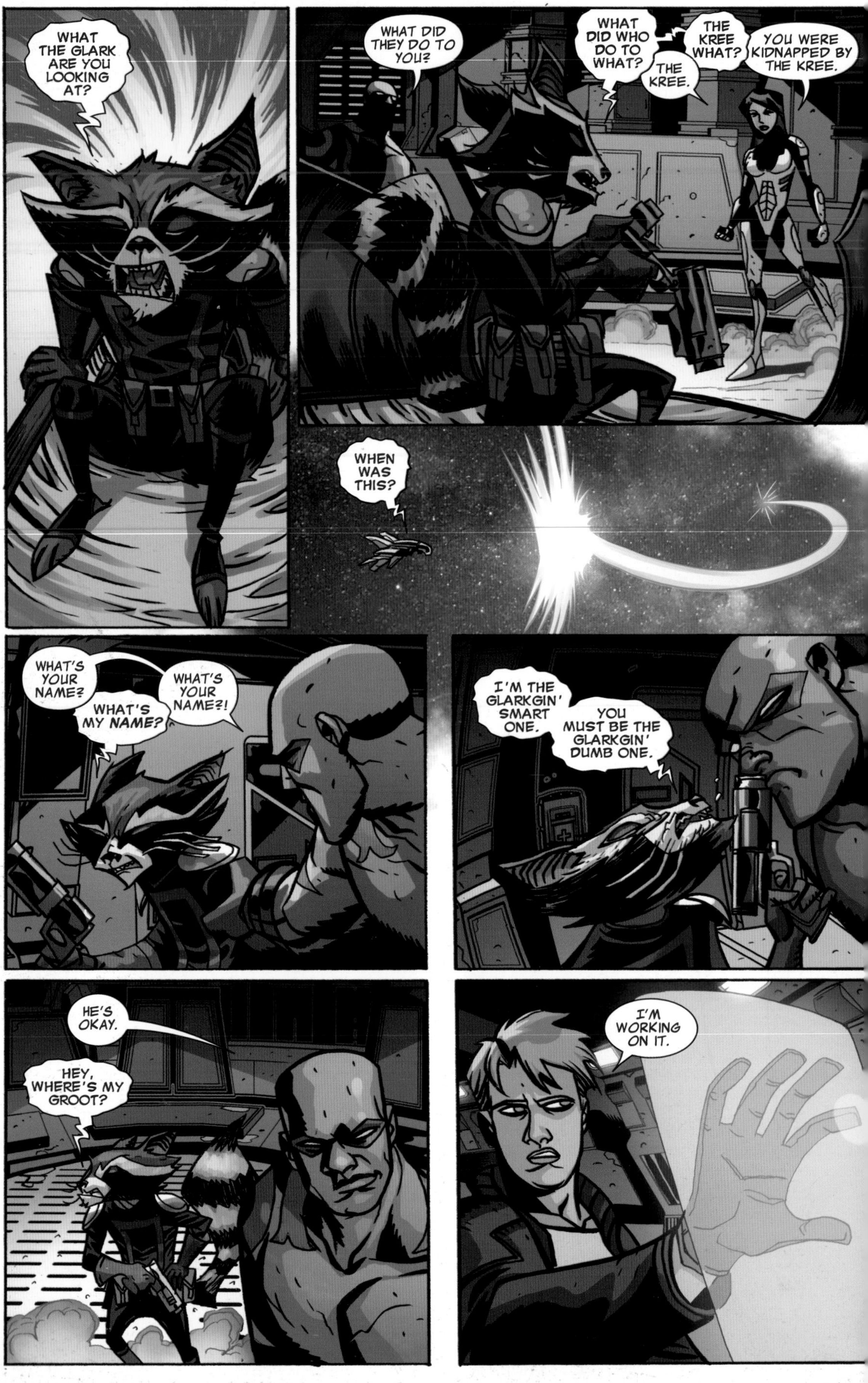
WHAT THE GLARK ARE YOU LOOKING AT?
WHAT DID THEY DO TO YOU?
WHAT DID WHO DO TO WHAT?
THE KREE.
THE KREE WHAT?
YOU WERE KIDNAPPED BY THE KREE.
WHEN WAS THIS?
WHAT'S YOUR NAME?
WHAT'S MY NAME?
WHAT'S YOUR NAME?!
I'M THE GLARKGIN' SMART ONE.
YOU MUST BE THE GLARKGIN' DUMB ONE.
HE'S OKAY.
HEY, WHERE'S MY GROOT?
I'M WORKING ON IT.

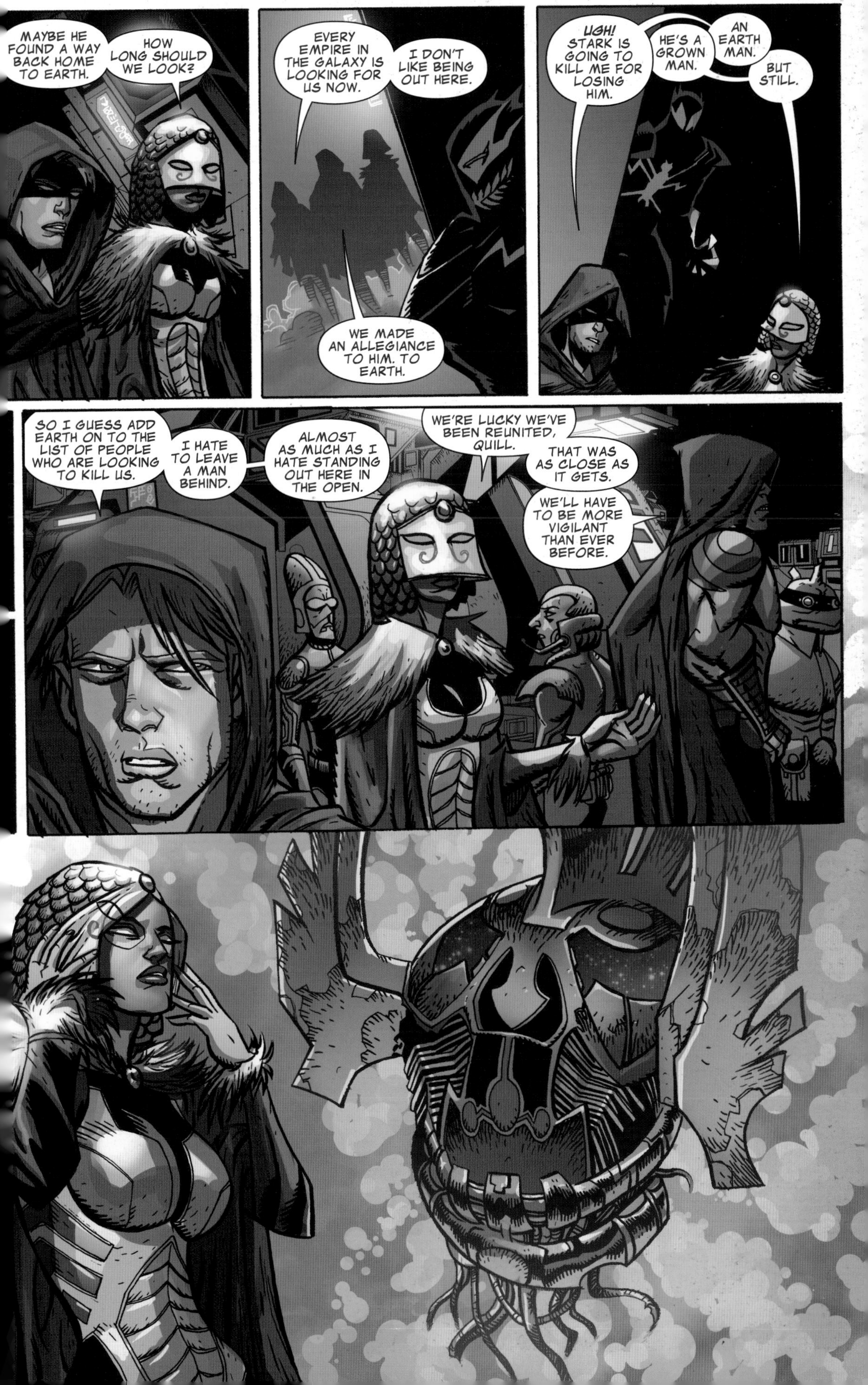
MAYBE HE FOUND A WAY BACK HOME TO EARTH.
HOW LONG SHOULD WE LOOK?
EVERY EMPIRE IN THE GALAXY IS LOOKING FOR US NOW.
I DON'T LIKE BEING OUT HERE.
WE MADE AN ALLEGIANCE TO HIM. TO EARTH.
UGH! STARK IS GOING TO KILL ME FOR LOSING HIM.
HE'S A GROWN MAN.
AN EARTH MAN.
BUT STILL.
SO I GUESS ADD EARTH ON TO THE LIST OF PEOPLE WHO ARE LOOKING TO KILL US.
I HATE TO LEAVE A MAN BEHIND.
ALMOST AS MUCH AS I HATE STANDING OUT HERE IN THE OPEN.
WE'RE LUCKY WE'VE BEEN REUNITED, QUILL.
THAT WAS AS CLOSE AS IT GETS.
WE'LL HAVE TO BE MORE VIGILANT THAN EVER BEFORE.

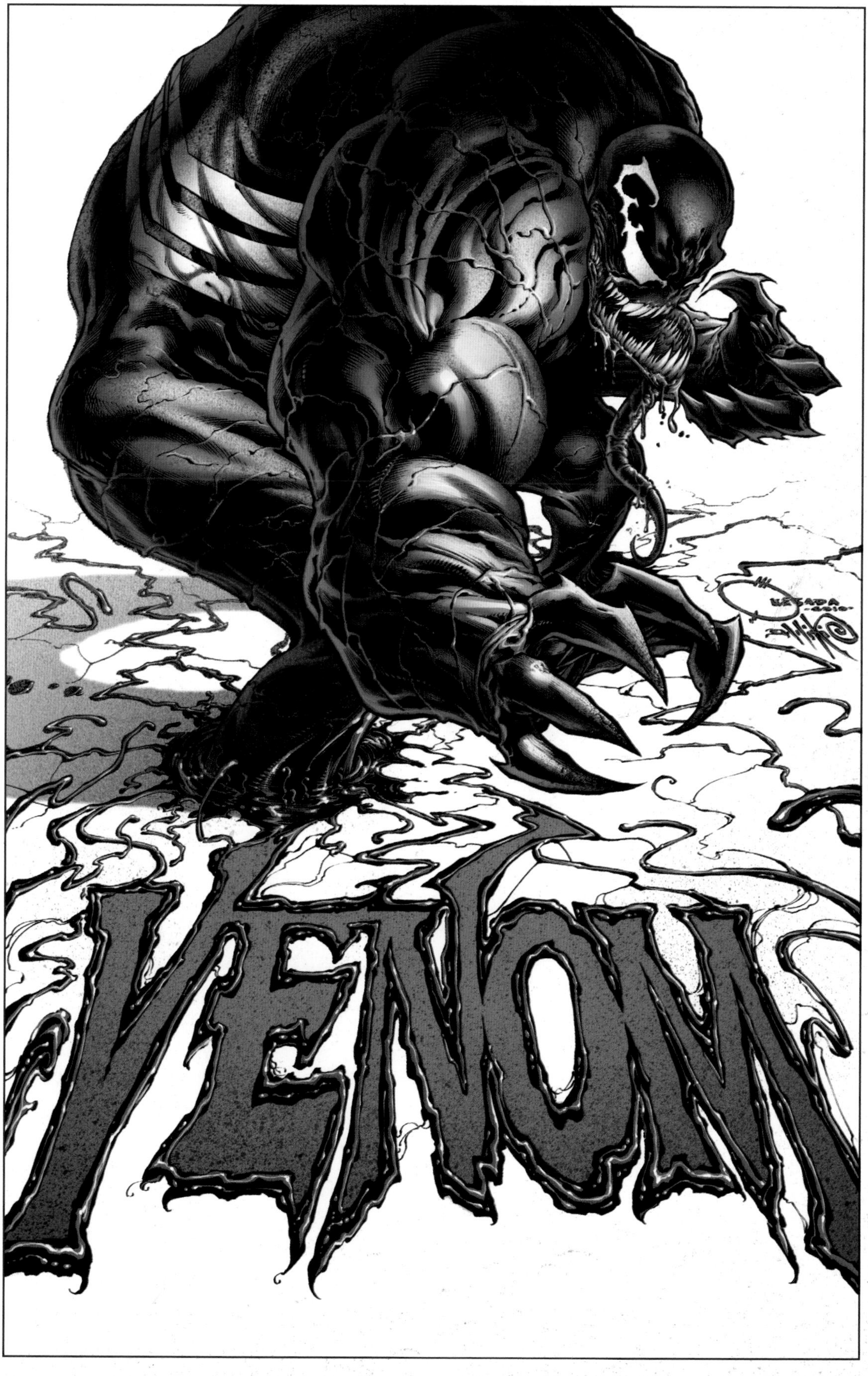
VENOM

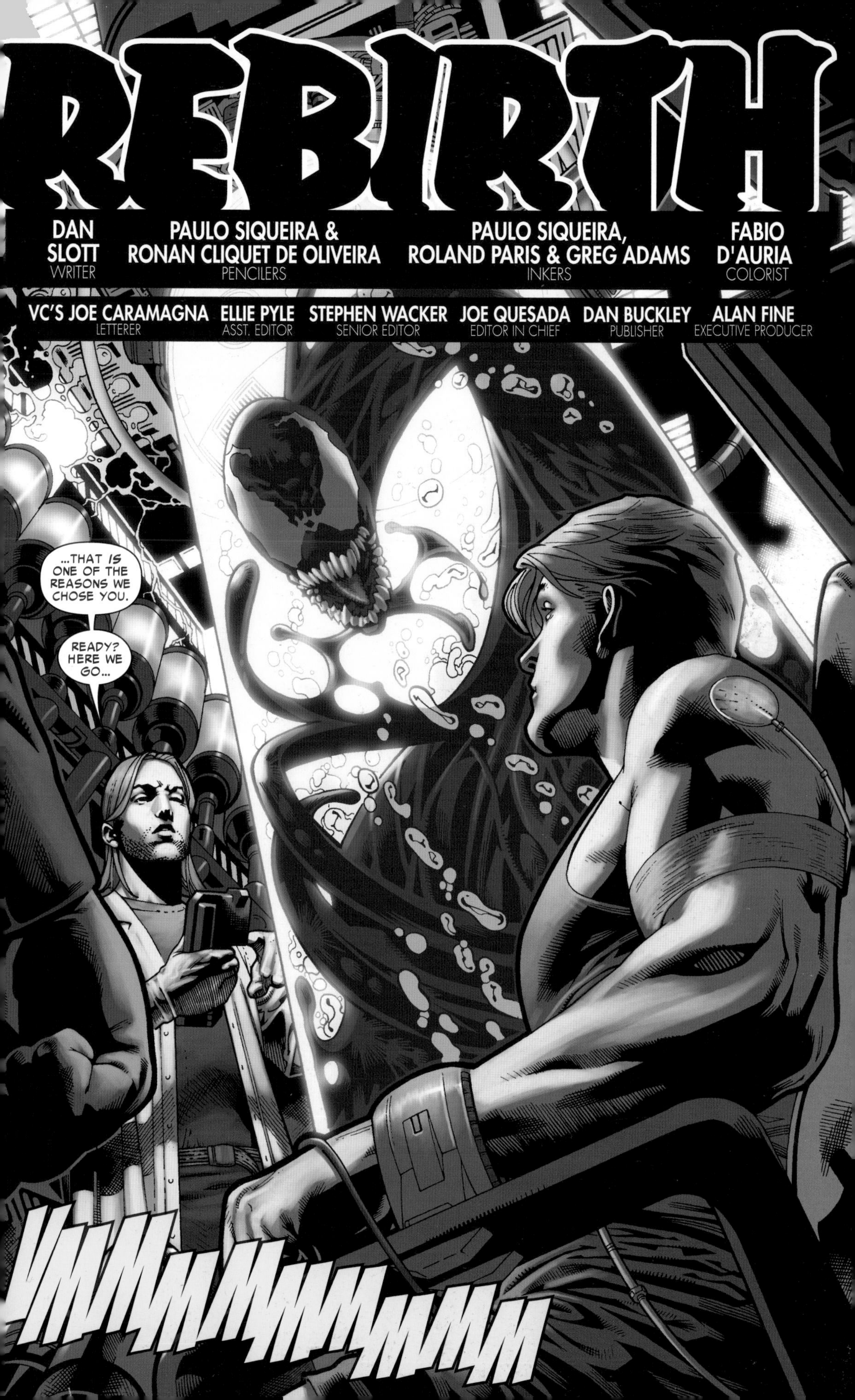
REBIRTH
DAN SLOTT WRITER
PAULO SIQUEIRA & RONAN CLIQUET DE OLIVEIRA PENCILERS
PAULO SIQUEIRA, ROLAND PARIS & GREG ADAMS INKERS
FABIO D'AURIA COLORIST
VC'S JOE CARAMAGNA LETTERER
ELLIE PYLE ASST. EDITOR
STEPHEN WACKER SENIOR EDITOR
JOE QUESADA EDITOR IN CHIEF
DAN BUCKLEY PUBLISHER
ALAN FINE EXECUTIVE PRODUCER
...THAT IS ONE OF THE REASONS WE CHOSE YOU.
READY? HERE WE GO...

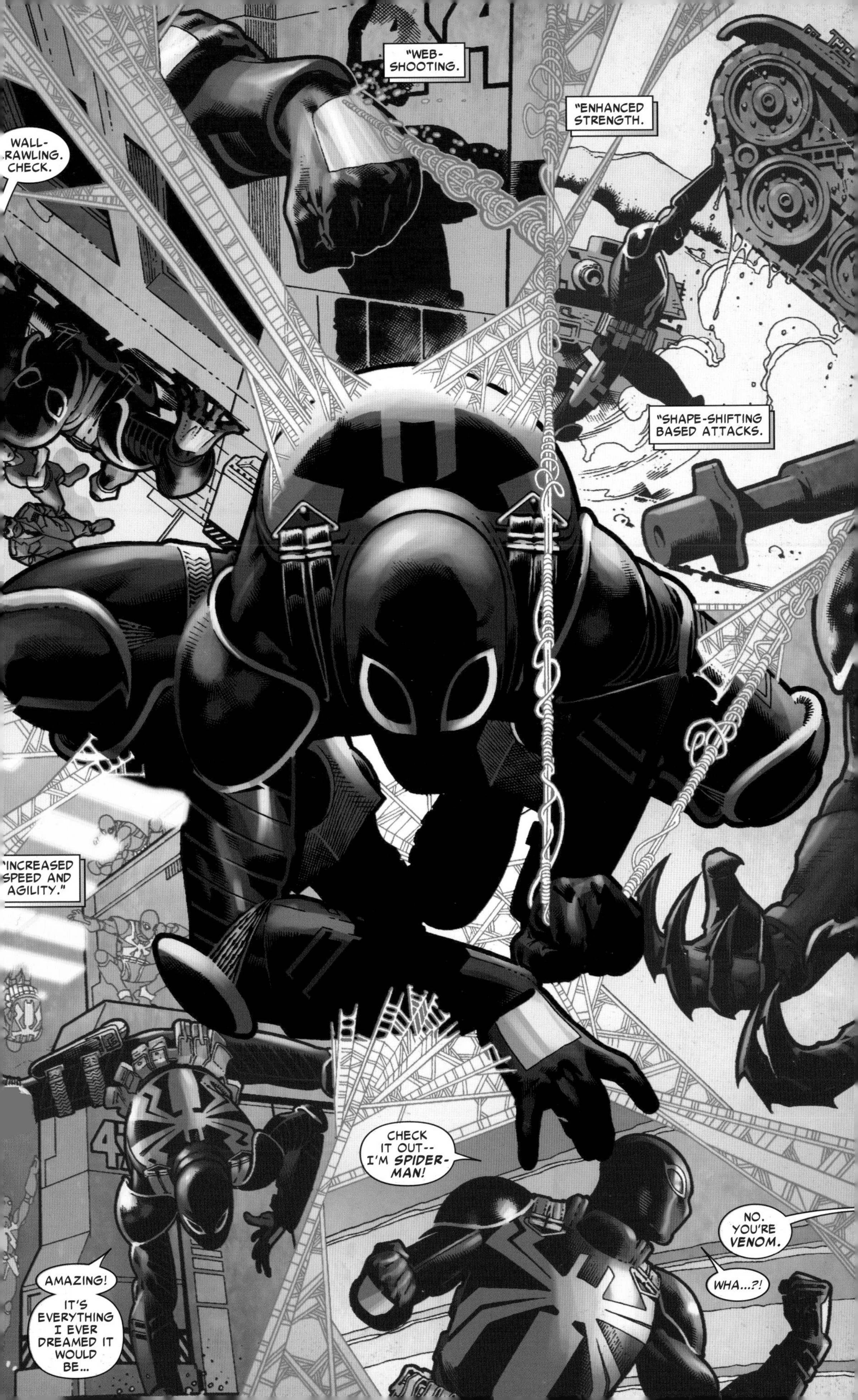
WALL-RAWLING. CHECK.
"WEB-SHOOTING.
"ENHANCED STRENGTH.
"SHAPE-SHIFTING BASED ATTACKS.
"INCREASED SPEED AND AGILITY."
CHECK IT OUT-- I'M SPIDER-MAN!
AMAZING!
IT'S EVERYTHING I EVER DREAMED IT WOULD BE...
NO. YOU'RE VENOM.
WHA...?!

WHY CAN'T I BE SPIDER-MAN? THERE'RE TWO HULKS, TWO CAPS, WHY CAN'T THERE BE TWO--

WE'RE SENDING YOU AFTER TERRORISTS. WE'VE DONE PSYCHE PROFILES. AND TERRORIST AREN'T AFRAID OF SPIDER-MAN.

SPEAKING OF THE KILLING...LET ME INTRODUCE YOU TO SOME OF YOUR NEW ORDNANCE...

THIS IS THE MULTI-GUN. SPECIALLY KEYED TO YOUR DNA. IT COST A LOT. DON'T LOSE IT.

KINDA CLUMSY FOR A STANDARD AUTOMATIC.

THEY KNOW HE DOESN'T KILL. VENOM, HOWEVER, WILL KILL YA, EAT YA, AND COME BACK FOR SECONDS.

WE'LL DENY IT, OF COURSE, BUT IT'LL GET OUT-- TO THE RIGHT CIRCLES. AND WHEN IT DOES, THAT'S A NICE REP TO HAVE.

SHKK

OH!

IT'S ALSO A HIGH-POWERED SNIPER RIFLE.

IT'S A FIREARM FOR EVERY OCCASION.

BUT NEVER FORGET, THAT SUIT--

--THE ALIEN SYMBIOTE, IS YOUR GREATEST WEAPON.

FLORP

BUT THESE WILL GIVE YOU A FEW MORE TRICKS UP YOUR SLEEVE.

WHAT ARE THEY?

KNOCKOUT DRUGS. TRUTH SERUM. AND CHEMICAL WEAPONS OF MY OWN DESIGN.

ALONG WITH VARIOUS KNIVES AND CUTTING TOOLS...

...THE SUIT CAN ALSO FASHION A SYRINGE AS A DELIVERY SYSTEM.

DANG, MACKENZIE. YOU GOT ME HOOKED UP WITH EVERYTHING THIS SIDE OF A SPIDER-SENSE.

YOU'VE GOT SOMETHING BETTER THAN THAT, THOMPSON. YOU'VE GOT ME.

UM... HULLO?

MARVEL GRAPHIC NOVEL

CAPTAIN MARVEL #1

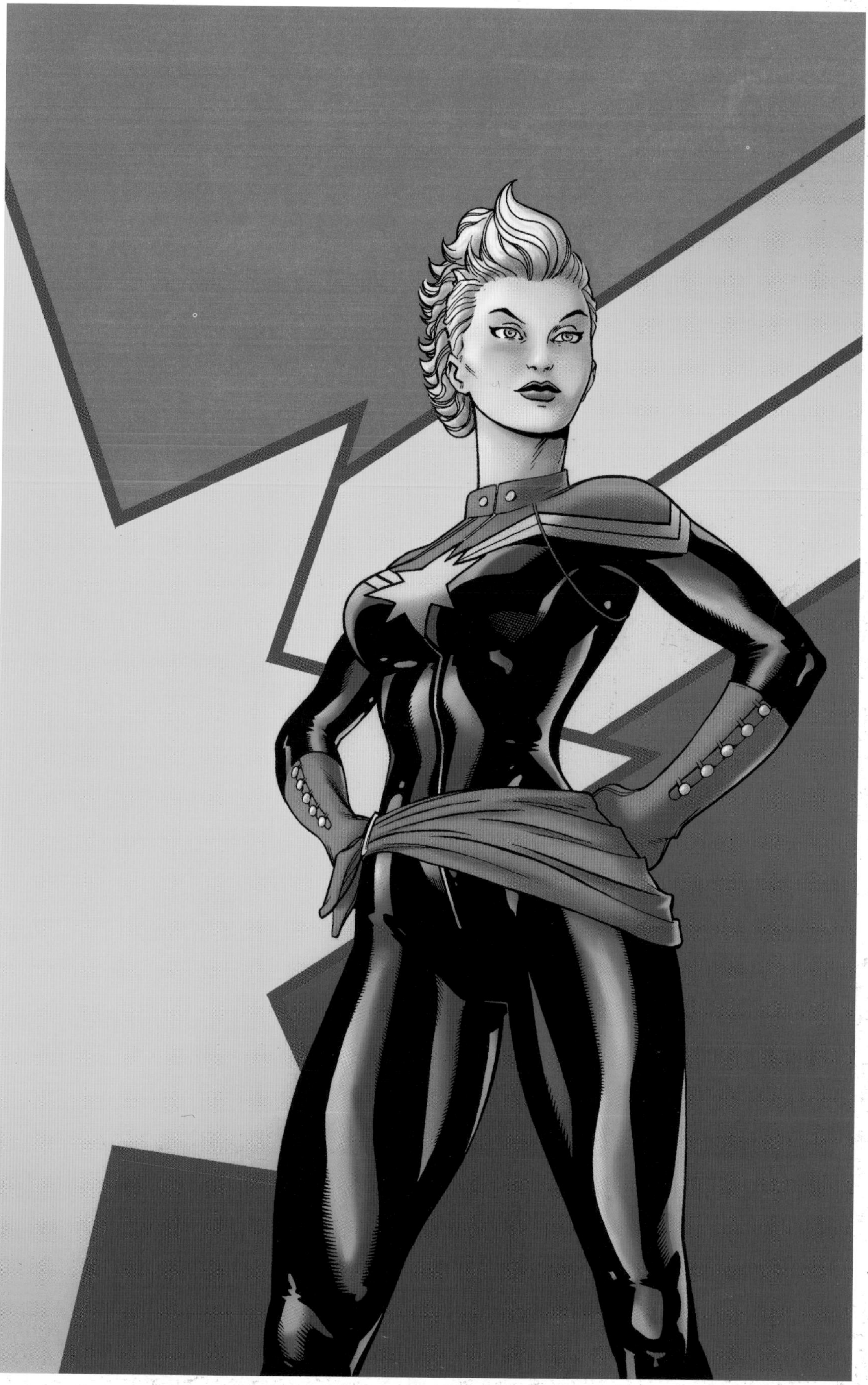

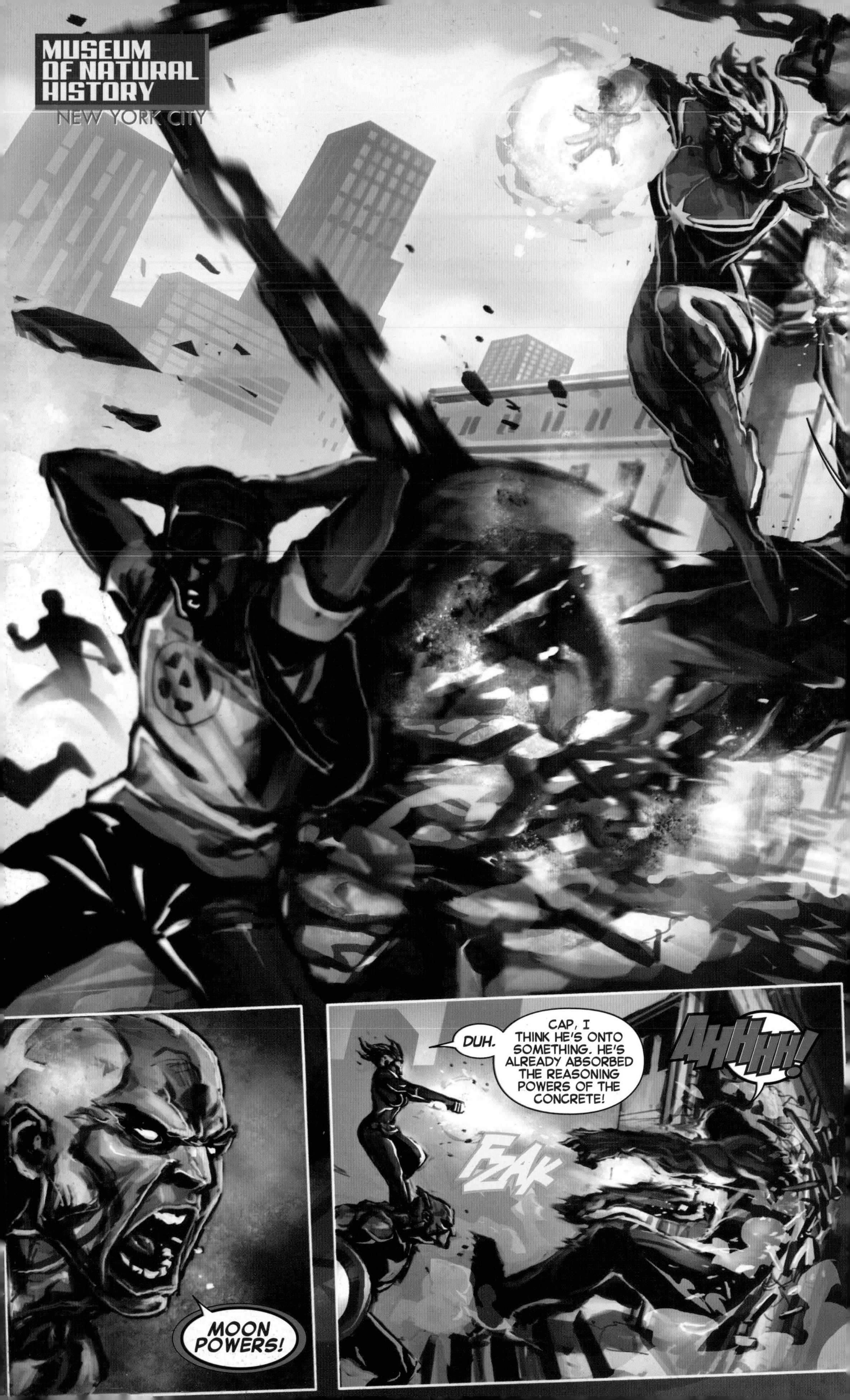

MUSEUM OF NATURAL HISTORY
NEW YORK CITY
MOON POWERS!
DUH.
CAP, I THINK HE'S ONTO SOMETHING. HE'S ALREADY ABSORBED THE REASONING POWERS OF THE CONCRETE!
AHHHH!
FZAK

THWUSHHHHHHHHHH

THREE SECONDS IN A MUSEUM AND YOU'RE SOUND ASLEEP.

WHY AM I NOT SURPRISED?

KCK

KCK

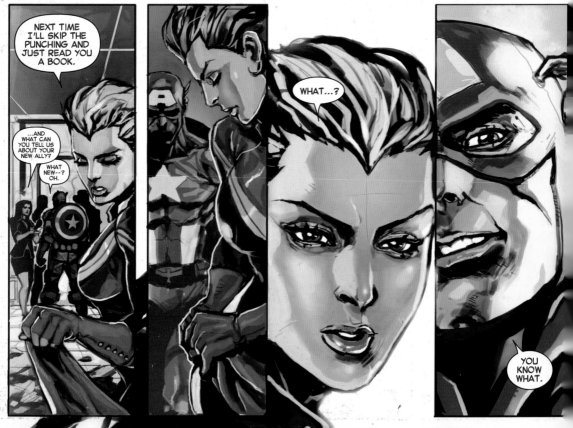

NEXT TIME I'LL SKIP THE PUNCHING AND JUST READ YOU A BOOK.

...AND WHAT CAN YOU TELL US ABOUT YOUR NEW ALLY?

WHAT NEW--? OH.

WHAT...?

YOU KNOW WHAT.

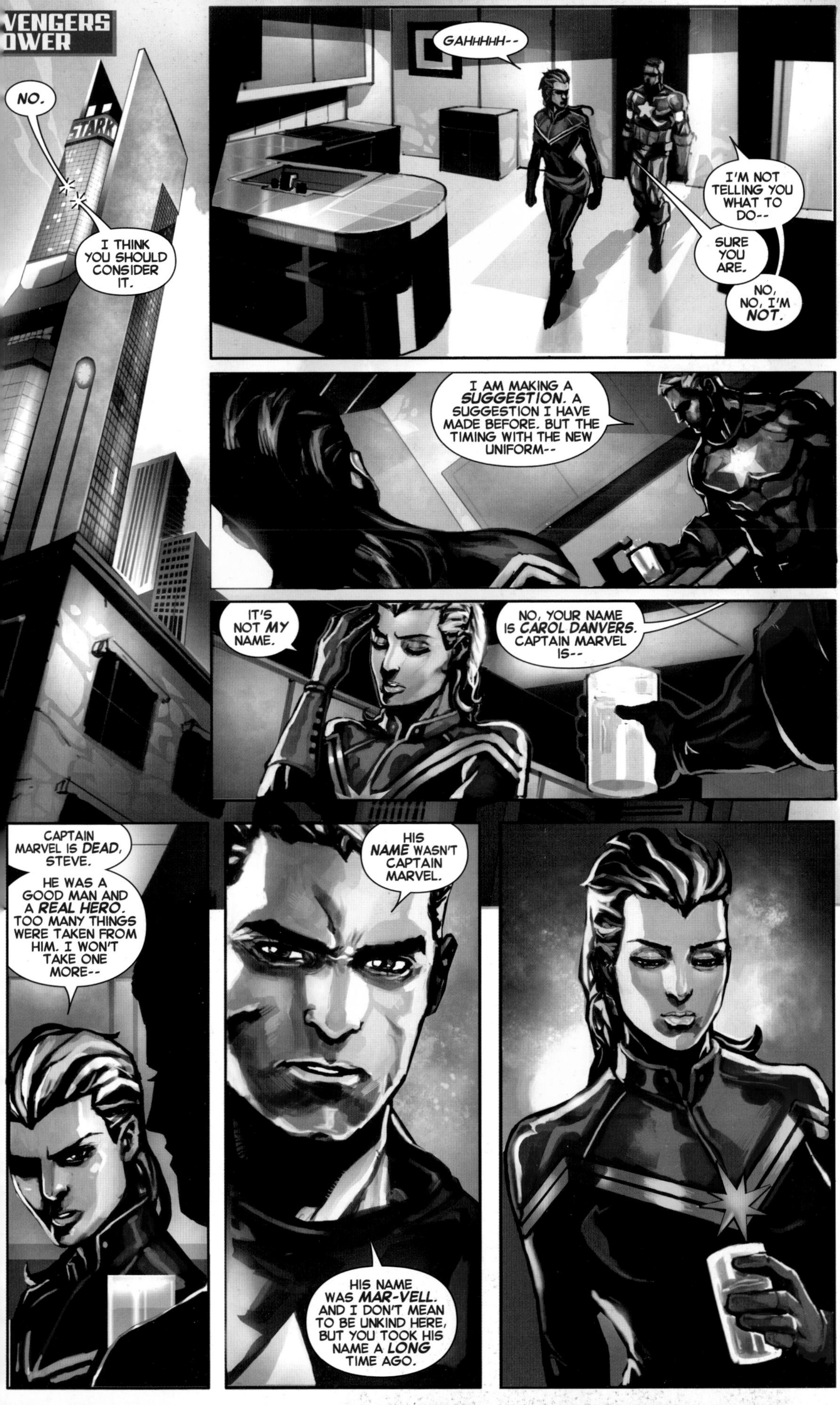
VENGERS
OWER
NO.
I THINK YOU SHOULD CONSIDER IT.
STARK
GAHHHHH--
I'M NOT TELLING YOU WHAT TO DO--
SURE YOU ARE.
NO, NO, I'M NOT.
I AM MAKING A SUGGESTION. A SUGGESTION I HAVE MADE BEFORE. BUT THE TIMING WITH THE NEW UNIFORM--
IT'S NOT MY NAME.
NO, YOUR NAME IS CAROL DANVERS. CAPTAIN MARVEL IS--
CAPTAIN MARVEL IS DEAD, STEVE.
HE WAS A GOOD MAN AND A REAL HERO. TOO MANY THINGS WERE TAKEN FROM HIM. I WON'T TAKE ONE MORE--
HIS NAME WASN'T CAPTAIN MARVEL.
HIS NAME WAS MAR-VELL. AND I DON'T MEAN TO BE UNKIND HERE, BUT YOU TOOK HIS NAME A LONG TIME AGO.

I WAS A LUCKY KID BECAUSE I HAD TWO HEROES--MY DAD AND A PILOT NAMED HELEN COBB.

HELEN HELD FIFTEEN SPEED RECORDS WHEN SHE RETIRED.

FIFTEEN.

I'M NOT PRONE TO ENVY. BUT THOSE RECORDS...

I ENVY THOSE RECORDS.

I CAN FLY. FAST.

REAL FAST.

BUT THESE "ABILITIES" COME AT A COST. FOR ONE THING, I'LL NEVER BE ALLOWED TO HOLD A RECORD LIKE HELEN'S.

I CAN'T EVEN COMPETE. WOULDN'T BE A FAIR FIGHT.

I LOST MY SHOT WHEN I WAS CAUGHT IN THE BLAST OF THAT ALIEN PSYCHE-MAGNETRON DEVICE.

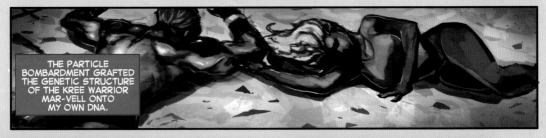

THE PARTICLE BOMBARDMENT GRAFTED THE GENETIC STRUCTURE OF THE KREE WARRIOR MAR-VELL ONTO MY OWN DNA.

IT'S A HELL OF A REWARD...BUT IT ERASED WHAT I LOVED MOST...

...THE RISK.

ONE MINUTE, FIFTY-EIGHT SECONDS FROM BROADWAY TO THE END OF OUR ATMOSPHERE, A NEW PERSONAL BEST.

LUCKY ME.

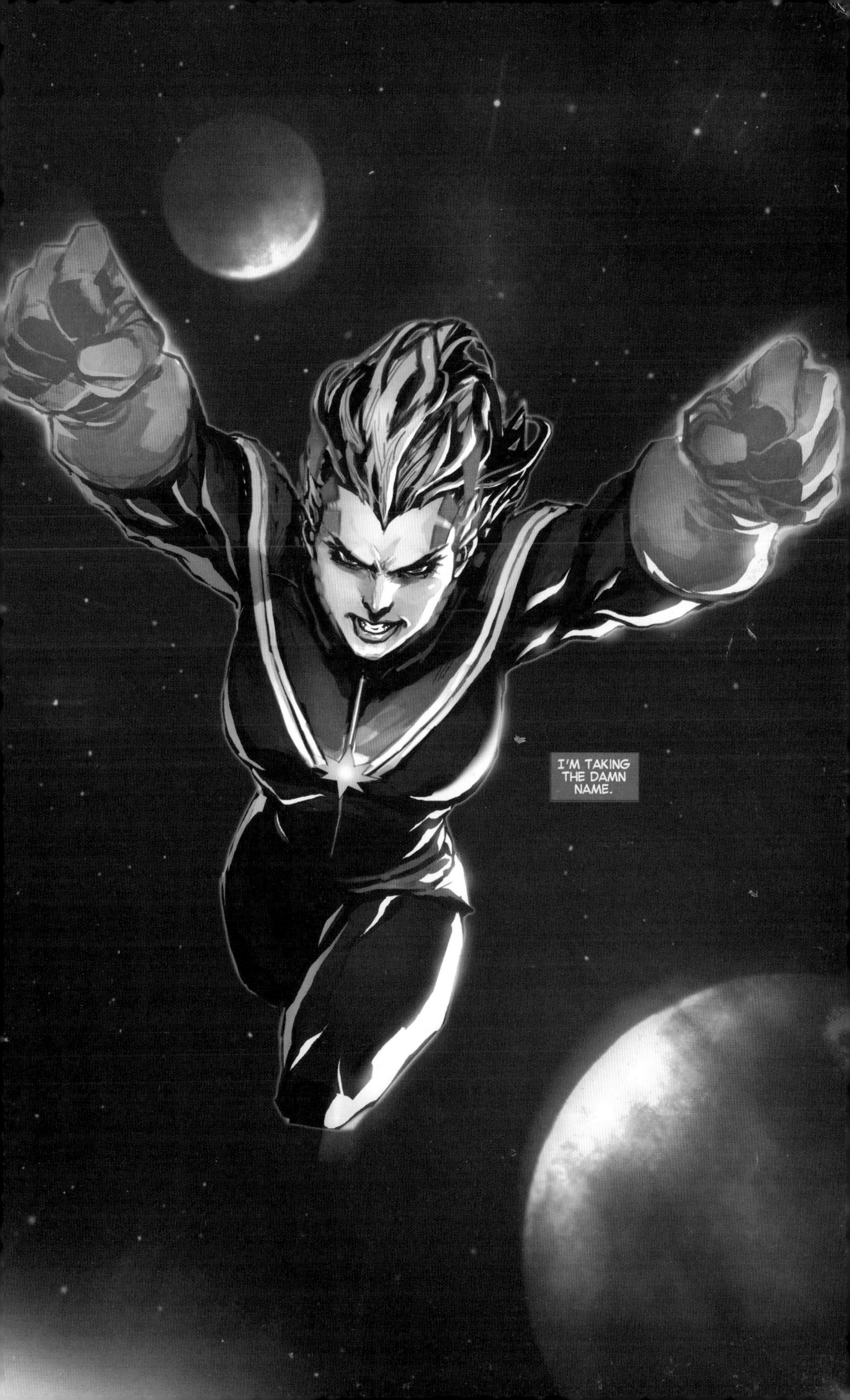
I'M TAKING THE DAMN NAME.

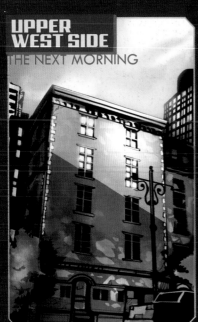

UPPER
WEST SIDE
THE NEXT MORNING

COFFEE, COFFEE...WHO HIDES THEIR COFFEE...?

WELL, HELLO, BEAUTIFUL.

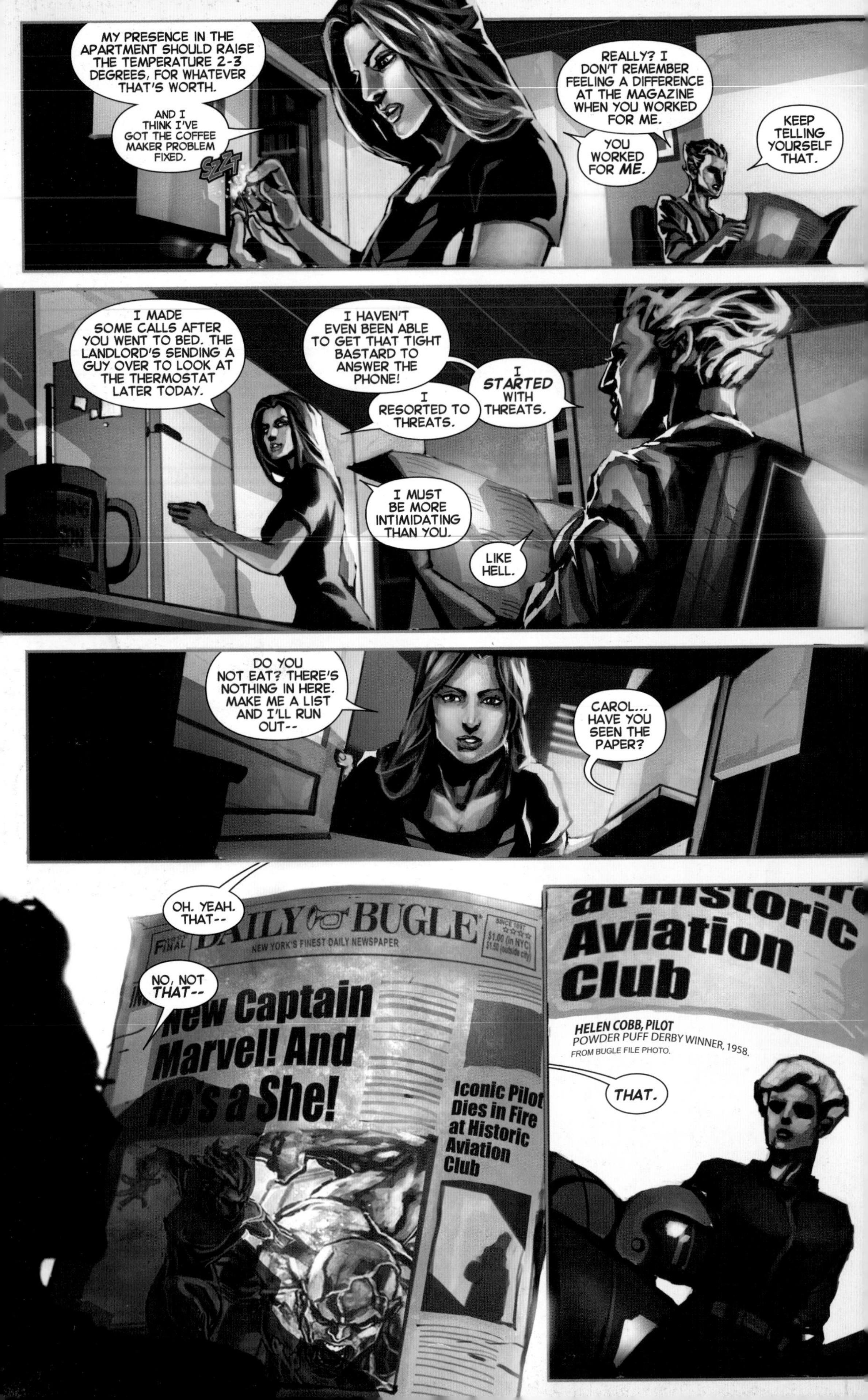
MY PRESENCE IN THE APARTMENT SHOULD RAISE THE TEMPERATURE 2-3 DEGREES, FOR WHATEVER THAT'S WORTH.
AND I THINK I'VE GOT THE COFFEE MAKER PROBLEM FIXED.
SZZT
REALLY? I DON'T REMEMBER FEELING A DIFFERENCE AT THE MAGAZINE WHEN YOU WORKED FOR ME.
YOU WORKED FOR ME.
KEEP TELLING YOURSELF THAT.
I MADE SOME CALLS AFTER YOU WENT TO BED. THE LANDLORD'S SENDING A GUY OVER TO LOOK AT THE THERMOSTAT LATER TODAY.
I HAVEN'T EVEN BEEN ABLE TO GET THAT TIGHT BASTARD TO ANSWER THE PHONE!
I STARTED WITH THREATS.
I RESORTED TO THREATS.
I MUST BE MORE INTIMIDATING THAN YOU.
LIKE HELL.
DO YOU NOT EAT? THERE'S NOTHING IN HERE. MAKE ME A LIST AND I'LL RUN OUT--
CAROL... HAVE YOU SEEN THE PAPER?
OH. YEAH. THAT--
DAILY BUGLE
FINAL
NEW YORK'S FINEST DAILY NEWSPAPER
SINCE 1897
$1.00 (in NYC) $1.50 (outside city)
NO, NOT THAT--
New Captain Marvel! And He's a She!
Iconic Pilot Dies in Fire at Historic Aviation Club
at Historic Aviation Club
HELEN COBB, PILOT
POWDER PUFF DERBY WINNER, 1958.
FROM BUGLE FILE PHOTO.
THAT.

Of higher, further, faster...more. Always more.

We came into the world spittin' mad, running full bore...

To or from what, I ain't never been able to tell.

I WAS JUST ADMIRING YOUR TROPHIES.

THAT'S WHAT THEY'RE THERE FOR. GOT 15 RECORDS TOTAL.

CAROL HERE'S IN AIR FORCE PILOT-TRAINING.

CAPTIVE AUDIENCE! HERE'S YOUR CHANCE. TELL HER WHAT YOU TOLD ME ABOUT YOUR ASTRONAUT DAYS--

YOU WERE IN THE MERCURY 13 PROGRAM?

TESTED AT THE SAME TIME AS JOHN GLENN. YOU CAN LOOK THAT UP.

NOW THOSE GALS--THOSE WERE SOME PILOTS. OUTSCORED THE SEVEN BOYS ON JUST ABOUT EVERY TEST WE TOOK.

WE'D'VE WIPED THE FLOOR WITH WHAT PASSES FOR A NINETY-NINER TODAY.

NO OFFENSE.

HEH. NONE TAKEN.

SALUT, THEN! I COMMEND YOU ON YOUR GOOD TASTE IN HEROES, KID.

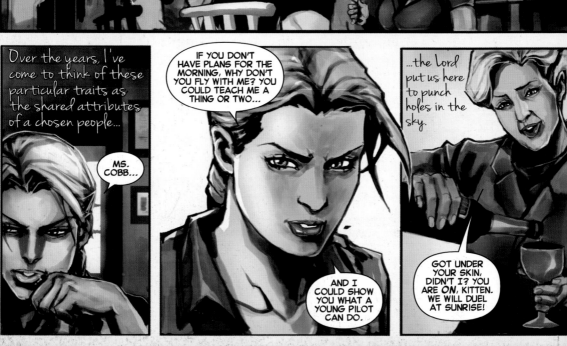

Over the years, I've come to think of these particular traits as the shared attributes of a chosen people...

MS. COBB...

IF YOU DON'T HAVE PLANS FOR THE MORNING, WHY DON'T YOU FLY WITH ME? YOU COULD TEACH ME A THING OR TWO...

AND I COULD SHOW YOU WHAT A YOUNG PILOT CAN DO.

...the Lord put us here to punch holes in the sky.

GOT UNDER YOUR SKIN, DIDN'T I? YOU ARE ON, KITTEN. WE WILL DUEL AT SUNRISE!

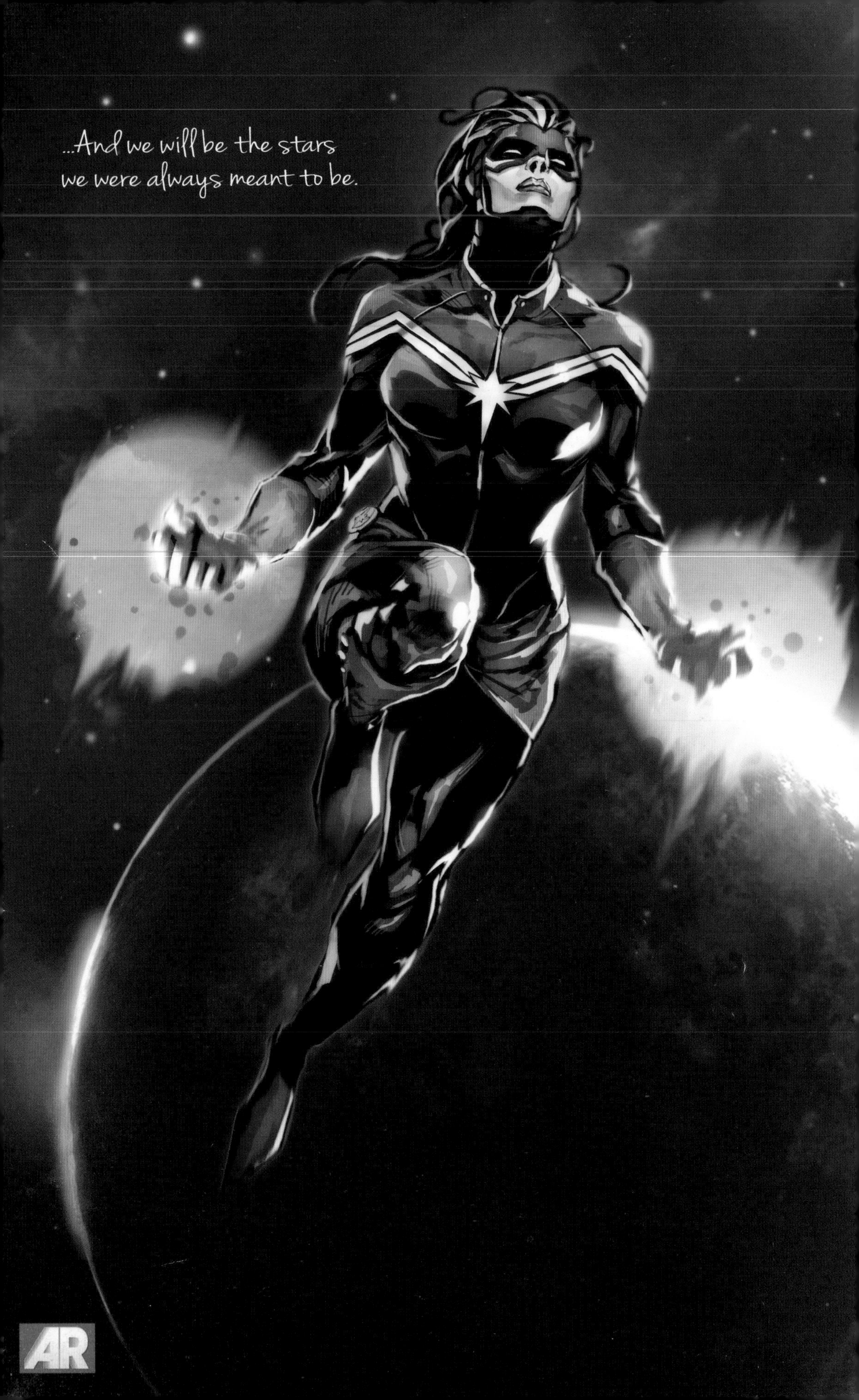
...And we will be the stars
we were always meant to be.

Variant Co

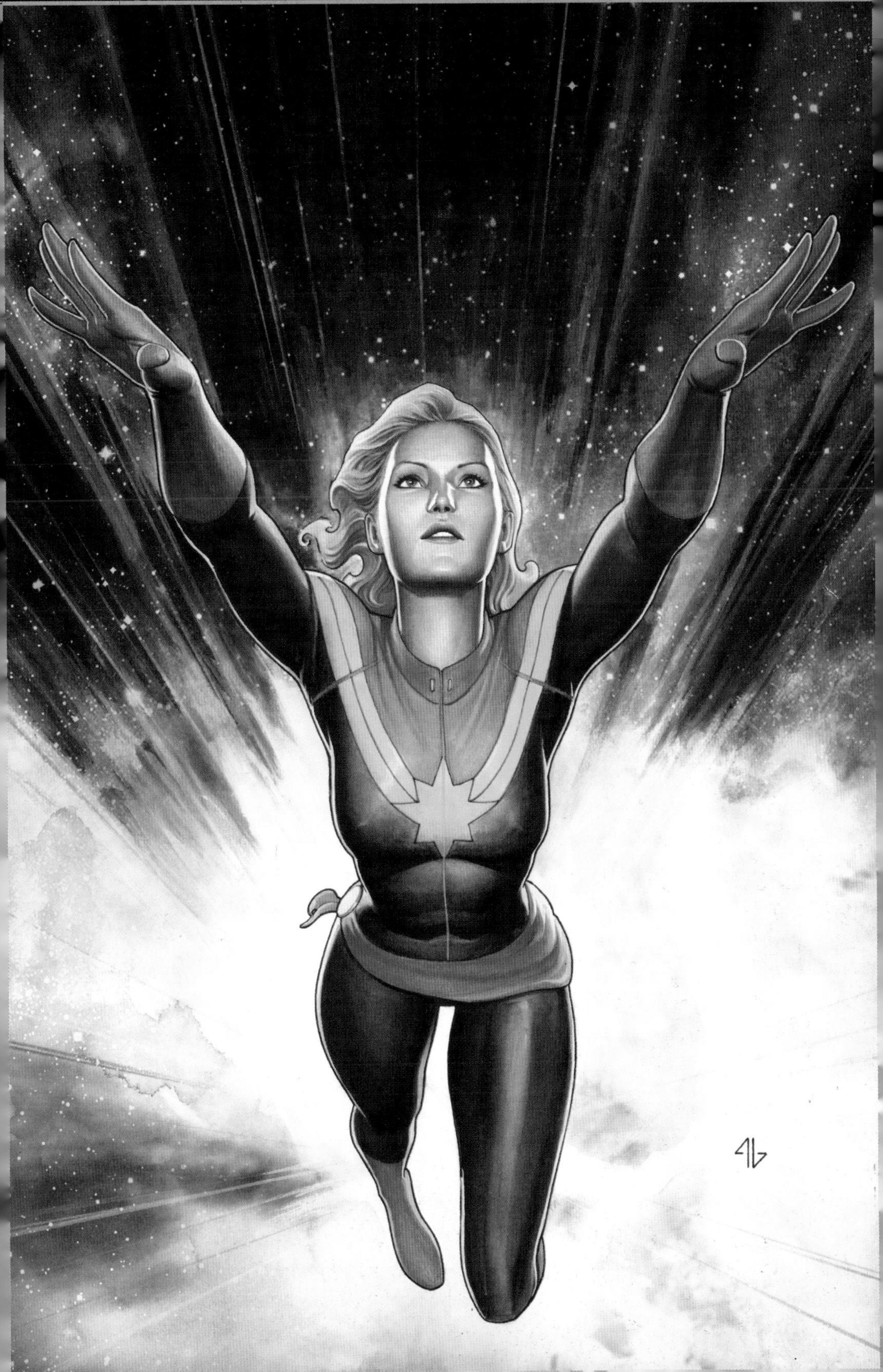

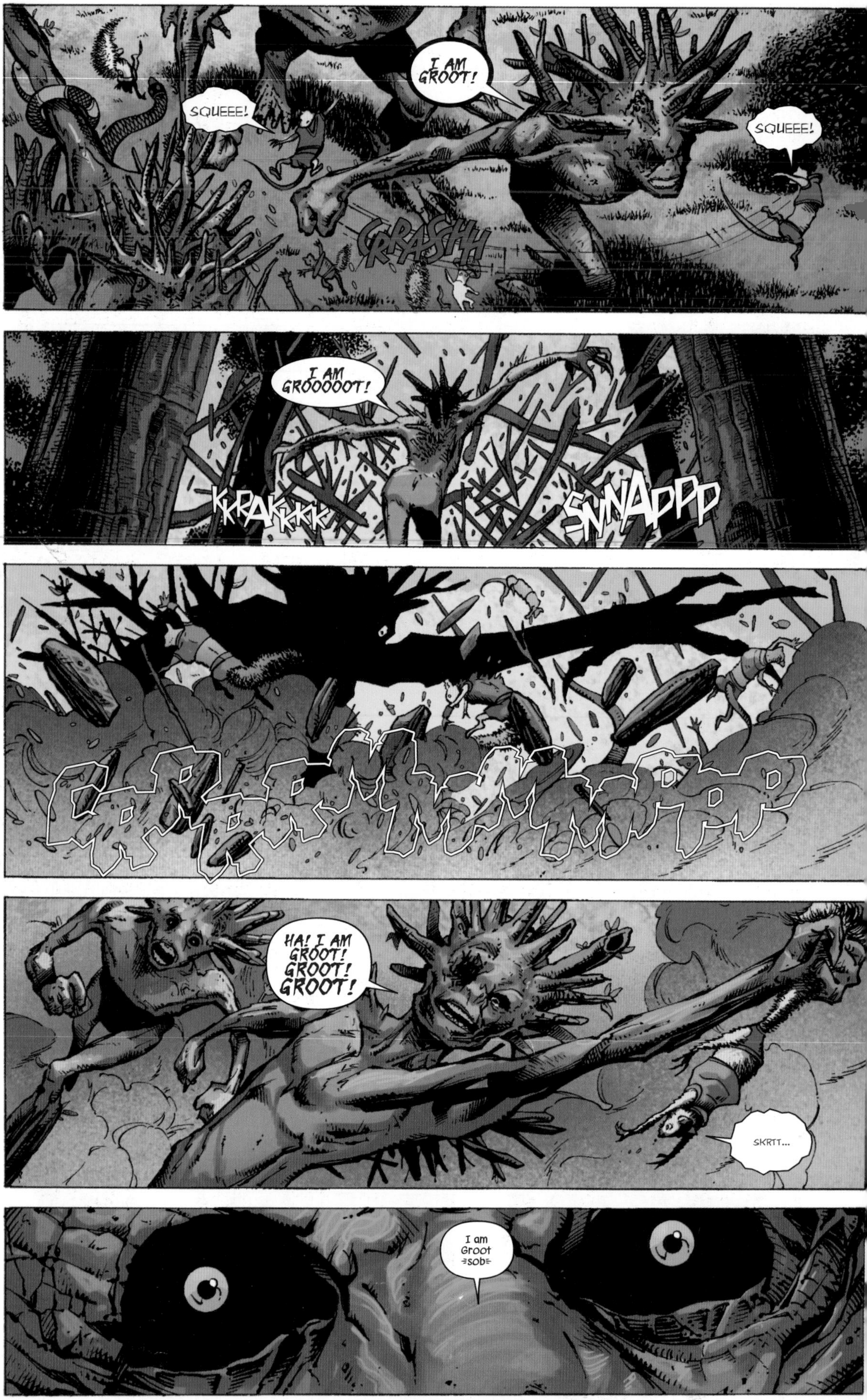
I AM GROOT!
SQUEEE!
SQUEEE!
CRASHHH
I AM GROOOOOT!
KKRAKKKKK
SNNAPPP
HA! I AM GROOT! GROOT! GROOT!
SKRTT...
I am Groot
=sob=

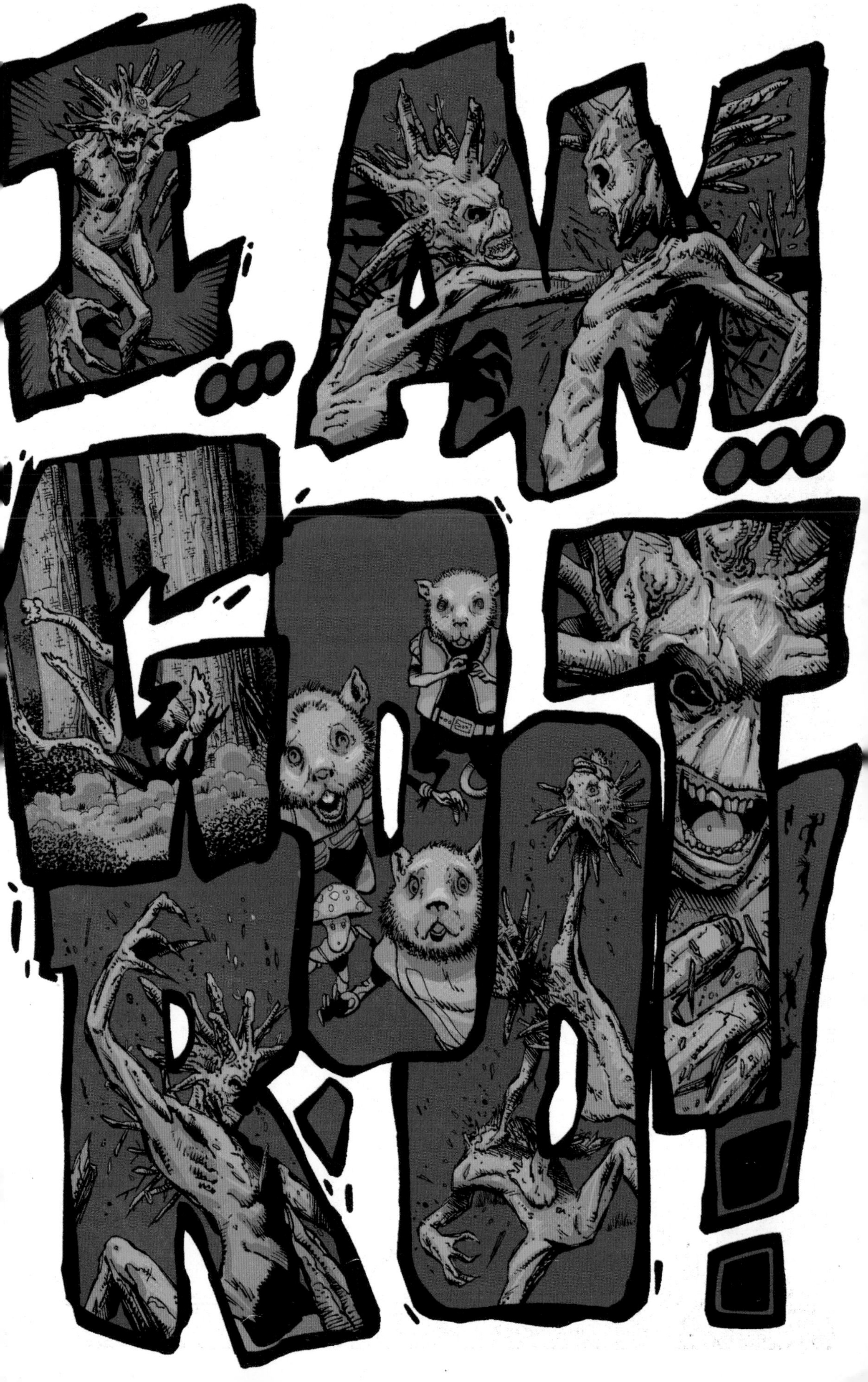
I... AM... GROOT!

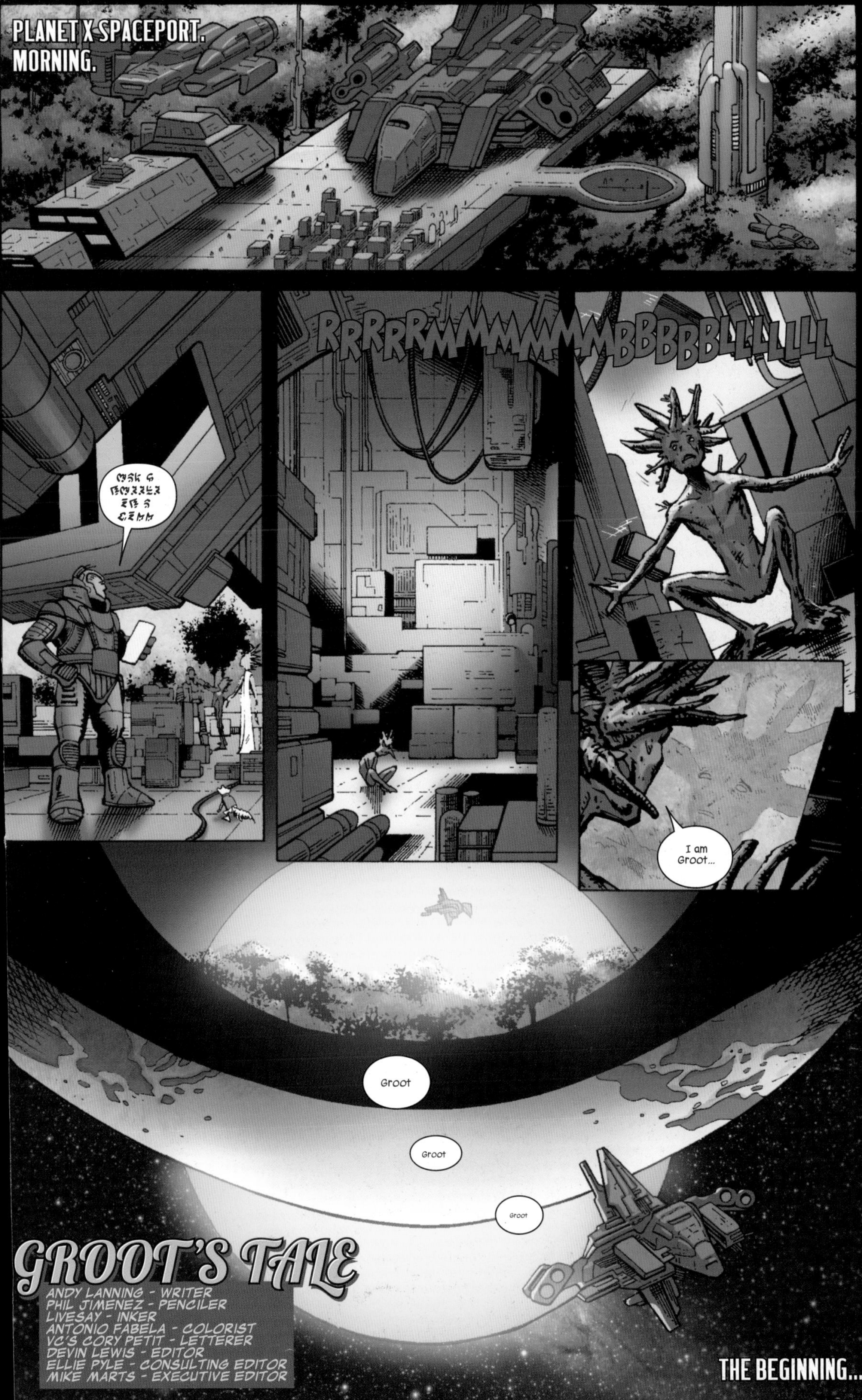
PLANET X SPACEPORT.
MORNING.
RRRRRMMMMMMMMBBBBBLLLLLLL
I am Groot...
Groot
Groot
Groot
GROOT'S TALE
ANDY LANNING - WRITER
PHIL JIMENEZ - PENCILER
LIVESAY - INKER
ANTONIO FABELA - COLORIST
VC'S CORY PETIT - LETTERER
DEVIN LEWIS - EDITOR
ELLIE PYLE - CONSULTING EDITOR
MIKE MARTS - EXECUTIVE EDITOR
THE BEGINNING...

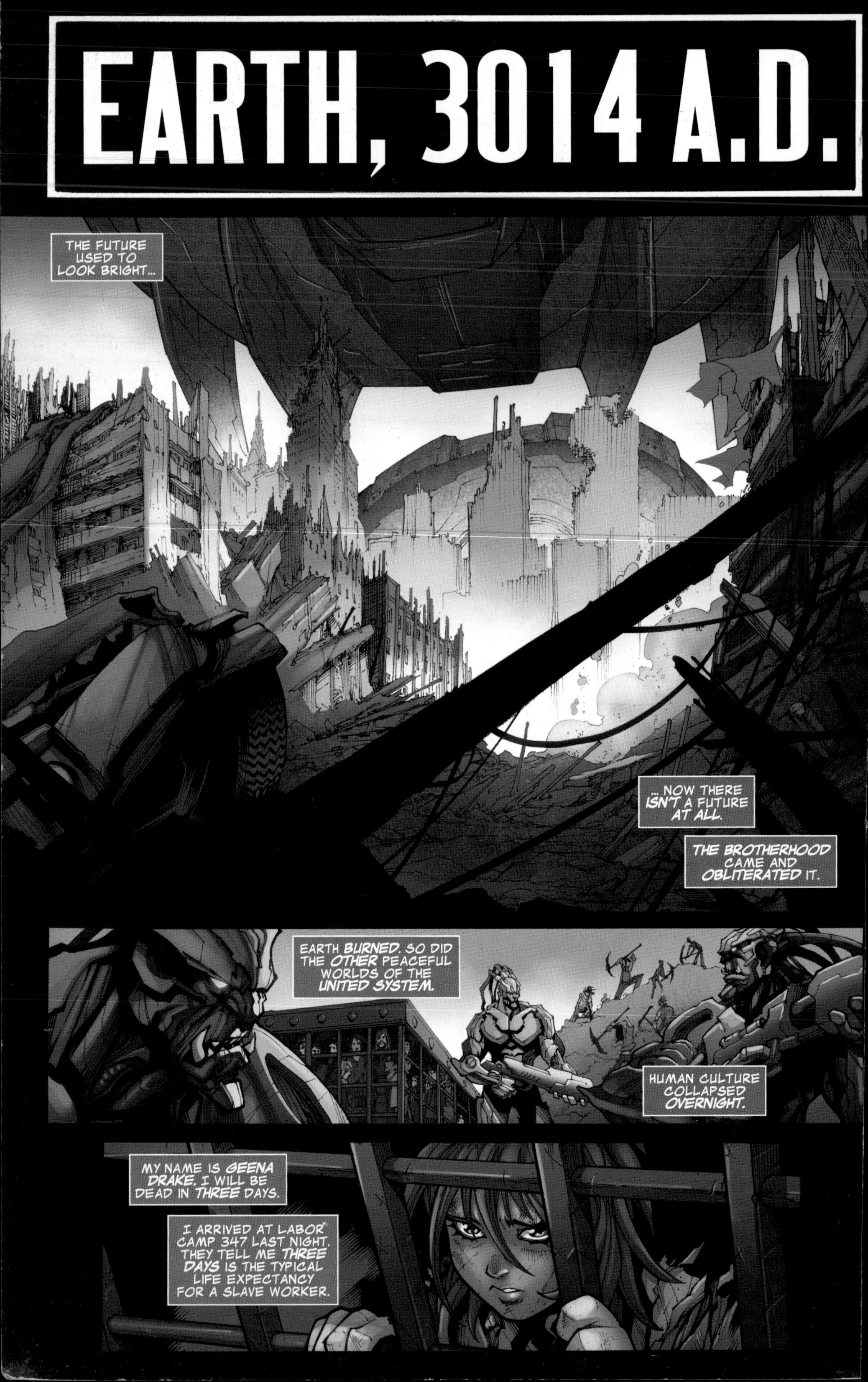
EARTH, 3014 A.D.
THE FUTURE USED TO LOOK BRIGHT...
... NOW THERE ISN'T A FUTURE AT ALL.
THE BROTHERHOOD CAME AND OBLITERATED IT.
EARTH BURNED. SO DID THE OTHER PEACEFUL WORLDS OF THE UNITED SYSTEM.
HUMAN CULTURE COLLAPSED OVERNIGHT.
MY NAME IS GEENA DRAKE. I WILL BE DEAD IN THREE DAYS.
I ARRIVED AT LABOR CAMP 347 LAST NIGHT. THEY TELL ME THREE DAYS IS THE TYPICAL LIFE EXPECTANCY FOR A SLAVE WORKER.

THE STORIES CALL HIM *VANCE ASTRO*.

THEY SAY HE IS A *THOUSAND* YEARS OLD, A MAN FROM ANOTHER AGE BROUGHT TO *OURS* BY SOME ACCIDENT OF CRYOGENIC SUSPENSION.

HE IS *NOT* A MAN.

HE IS A *BLUR*.

WHAT HIS BLOWS DO NOT FELL--

HE MOVES WITH *IMPOSSIBLE* AGILITY, HIS MOVEMENTS BOOSTED AND ENHANCED BY PSIONIC IMPULSES.

--HIS MIND *LEVELS*.

HE CARRIES THE SHIELD OF AN *ANCIENT HERO*. IT REPRESENTS AN *IDEAL*.

IT IS A SYMBOL OF *LIBERTY* AND *EQUALITY* FOR THE *ENTIRE* UNITED SYSTEM.

GUARDIANS!

AGAIN, THE PSIONIC CALL.

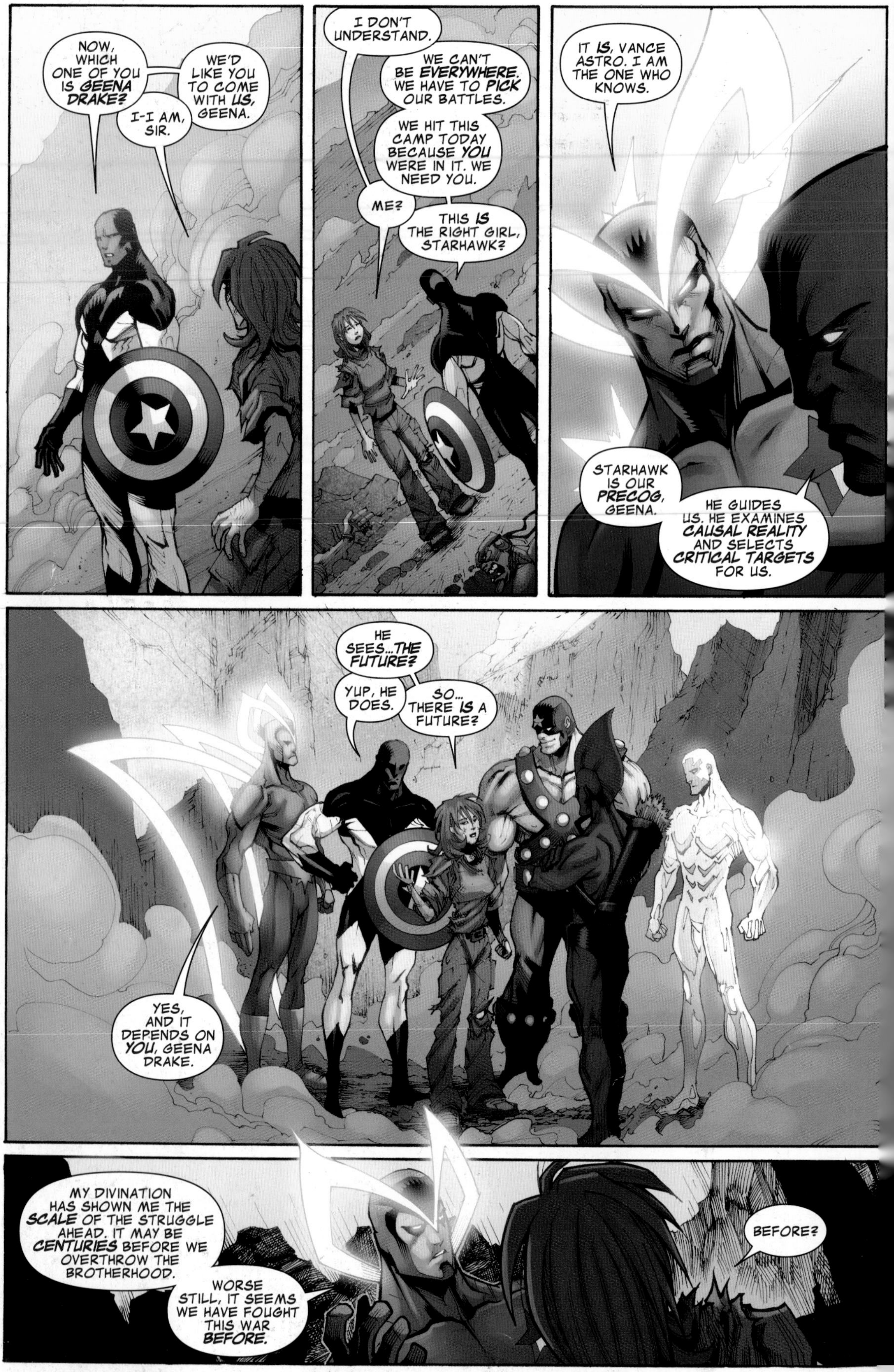
NOW, WHICH ONE OF YOU IS GEENA DRAKE?
WE'D LIKE YOU TO COME WITH US, GEENA.
I-I AM, SIR.
I DON'T UNDERSTAND.
WE CAN'T BE EVERYWHERE. WE HAVE TO PICK OUR BATTLES.
WE HIT THIS CAMP TODAY BECAUSE YOU WERE IN IT. WE NEED YOU.
ME?
THIS IS THE RIGHT GIRL, STARHAWK?
IT IS, VANCE ASTRO. I AM THE ONE WHO KNOWS.
STARHAWK IS OUR PRECOG, GEENA.
HE GUIDES US. HE EXAMINES CAUSAL REALITY AND SELECTS CRITICAL TARGETS FOR US.
HE SEES...THE FUTURE?
YUP, HE DOES.
SO... THERE IS A FUTURE?
YES, AND IT DEPENDS ON YOU, GEENA DRAKE.
MY DIVINATION HAS SHOWN ME THE SCALE OF THE STRUGGLE AHEAD. IT MAY BE CENTURIES BEFORE WE OVERTHROW THE BROTHERHOOD.
WORSE STILL, IT SEEMS WE HAVE FOUGHT THIS WAR BEFORE.
BEFORE?

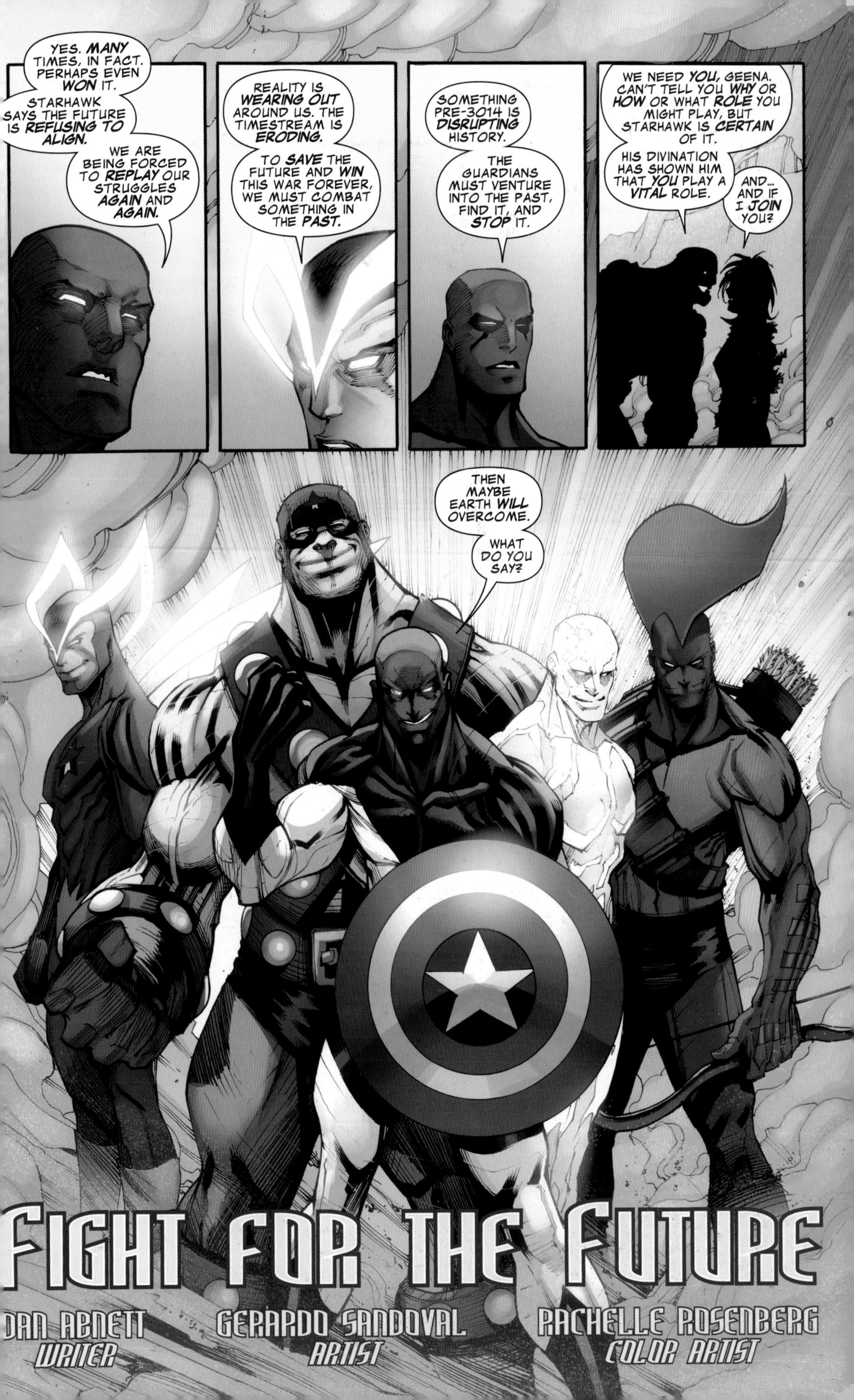
YES. MANY TIMES, IN FACT. PERHAPS EVEN WON IT.
STARHAWK SAYS THE FUTURE IS REFUSING TO ALIGN.
WE ARE BEING FORCED TO REPLAY OUR STRUGGLES AGAIN AND AGAIN.
REALITY IS WEARING OUT AROUND US. THE TIMESTREAM IS ERODING.
TO SAVE THE FUTURE AND WIN THIS WAR FOREVER, WE MUST COMBAT SOMETHING IN THE PAST.
SOMETHING PRE-3014 IS DISRUPTING HISTORY.
THE GUARDIANS MUST VENTURE INTO THE PAST, FIND IT, AND STOP IT.
WE NEED YOU, GEENA. CAN'T TELL YOU WHY OR HOW OR WHAT ROLE YOU MIGHT PLAY, BUT STARHAWK IS CERTAIN OF IT.
HIS DIVINATION HAS SHOWN HIM THAT YOU PLAY A VITAL ROLE.
AND... AND IF I JOIN YOU?
THEN MAYBE EARTH WILL OVERCOME.
WHAT DO YOU SAY?
FIGHT FOR THE FUTURE
DAN ABNETT
WRITER
GERARDO SANDOVAL
ARTIST
RACHELLE ROSENBERG
COLOR ARTIST

Variant Cover

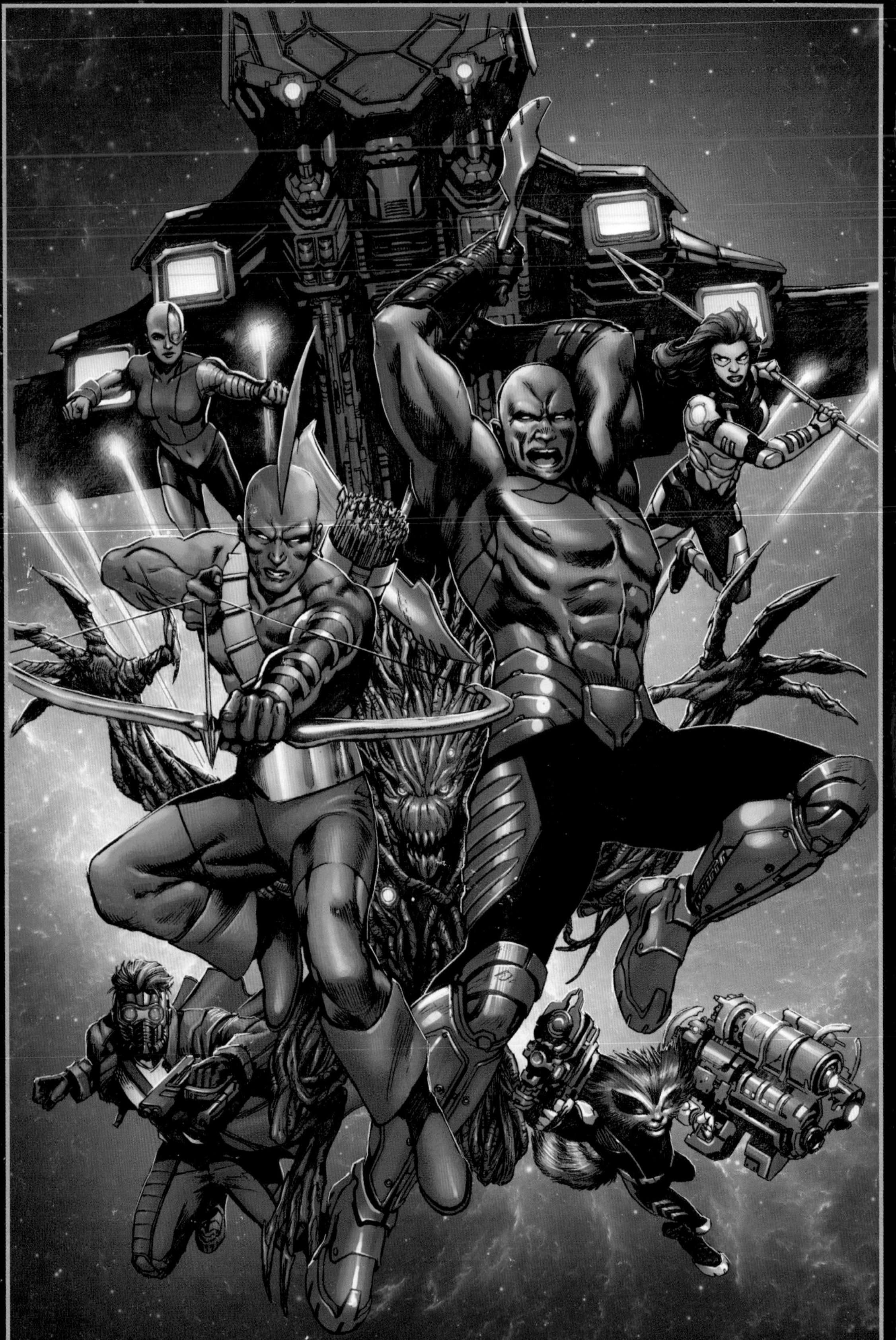

Guardians of the Galaxy #17
Variant by Alvaro Martinez